SECRETS OF FINDING
UNCLAIMED MONEY

SECRETS OF FINDING UNCLAIMED MONEY

Richard S. Johnson

First Edition

MIE PUBLISHING

MIE Publishing
PO Box 17118
Spartanburg, SC 29301
(800) 937-2133

Alternative Cataloging in Publication Data:

Johnson, Richard S., 1933-
     Secrets of Finding Unclaimed Money. Spartanburg, SC: MIE Publishing, copyright 1996.
     PARTIAL CONTENTS: Unclaimed money. How to obtain money from private businesses and financial institutions. From state Unclaimed Property Offices. Through probate courts. From the federal government. -Professional heir searching. Heir searching as a profession. State requirements for heir searchers.
     APPENDICES: Directory of Unclaimed Property Offices. -Locator services. -Computer access programs. - Bibliography. -Glossary.

     1. Unclaimed money. 2. Unclaimed estates. 3. State Unclaimed Property Offices—Directories. 4. Heir searching. I. Title. II. Title: Finding unclaimed money. III. Title: Unclaimed money finding. IV. MIE Publishing

332.02401

ISBN #1-877639-40-0

DISCLAIMER

Acknowledgements

I wish to acknowledge the enormous contributions made by Julie Delpho, Debbie Knox, and Libby Lindsey, for months of painstaking assistance. Special thanks are due to Tom Ninkovich for his editing and to George Foster for his cover design.

How to Use This Book

This book was written to be understood with as little effort as possible. Every attempt was made to use the simplest and clearest terms possible. However, since some of the subject matter may be technical or not commonly known, it is advisable to become familiar with the glossary and case study sections. This book is divided into two parts. Part I (Chapters 1-5) explains what you can do to locate and obtain money that may be due you or a member of your family. Chapter 1 explains what unclaimed money is. Chapter 2 deals with money currently held by private companies and financial organizations. Chapter 3 explains how to find out if you have money held in state Unclaimed Property Offices. It also includes the addresses and phone numbers for each office. Chapter 4 deals with money held by probate courts. Chapter 5 provides information about unclaimed money held by the federal government. At the end of Chapters 2-5 are actual case studies showing various examples.

Part II (Chapters 6-9) explains how you can have a profitable career as an heir searcher. Chapter 6 gives a thorough explanation of heir searching. It describes what you can do to find money that belongs to others and how to obtain finder's fees. Chapter 7 details what each state requires of heir searchers. Chapter 8 concerns contracts and agreements. Chapter 9 contains case studies solved using the procedures discussed in this book. If your interest is to become an heir searcher, you should familiarize yourself with the entire book, not just with Part II.

No matter the reason for using this book, it can definitely show you how to find abandoned and unclaimed money. Use it carefully and it should be of great assistance to you. The information and procedures listed have proven to be profitable. Good luck in your searching.

TABLE OF CONTENTS

The Purpose of This Book

This book is about finding money and other assets that are unclaimed or have been abandoned. Today there is over $40 billion of such assets in the United States. This is the net worth of the 4 richest men in the world.

According to an article in Forbes Magazine, chances are that one person in ten has unclaimed money. The average recipient receives around $700, but many receive more—some receive millions of dollars.

There are many reasons why money is abandoned or unclaimed. The main ones are:

1. The owner dies and no one else knows about the money.

2. The owner dies and the heirs cannot be found.

3. The owner has forgotten about the money.

4. The owners/heirs are unaware of their right to claim the money. For example, when there is no will, the estate goes to the next of kin. However, the term "next of kin" is defined by each state. In some cases, cousins, nieces, nephews or other blood relatives may legally claim an inheritance.

It is hard to believe that people forget about money, but it happens and the amounts are not always small. Many times the claims are more than $100,000.

The rightful owner or their heirs can claim this money, but very few do. It's fairly easy to find out if you or your family has money due. This book shows you where to look and how to get this money.

This book also explains how you can have a profitable career as an heir searcher. There are big finder's fees available for people who locate the owners or heirs to abandoned and unclaimed money.

Part I

Unclaimed Money

Chapter One

Unclaimed money—the basics

The origin of unclaimed money laws dates back to English Common Law, when all abandoned money and assets became the property of the King. The American colonies adopted this principle of Common Law known as the law of "escheat." When the colonies became the United States, each state retained this principle of escheat so that unclaimed and abandoned property became the property of that state.

All 50 states, plus the District of Columbia, currently have escheat laws. These laws are all similar, but differ in abandonment period and the specific assets that must be turned over to the state. All states allow the rightful owners or heirs to reclaim the money from the state. The laws also differ in the percentage heir searchers may obtain for locating missing heirs or owners of money held by the states. The federal government does not have escheat laws.

Under the law of escheat, depository institutions (banks, savings and loan associations, and credit unions) are required to turn over to the state all accounts that have been inactive for a certain period of time. This period varies depending on the type of property but is usually five to seven years. This applies to all types of accounts as well as items in safe deposit boxes. Once money reaches the state, it become absolutely dormant, accumulating no interest. The exception is Virginia which pays up to 5% on interest bearing accounts.

State Unclaimed Property Offices

Each state has an Unclaimed Property Office. When an asset is turned over to the state, it becomes an Unclaimed Property Office account. This office is responsible for maintaining the list of all unclaimed property accounts and for processing claims for these assets.

Many different types of assets are turned over to the state Unclaimed Property Office. Most are from financial institutions such as banks, credit unions and savings and loans. These unclaimed assets total in the billions of dollars and are growing each day because only a small percentage of owners come forward to make a claim. States expect to return only a small percentage of these total funds and usually keep a small reserve for this purpose. The rest is used to operate the state governments.

Some states hold tangible (material) assets, such as contents of safe deposit boxes or valuable items left in storage, and allow them to be claimed in the same manner as intangible (nonmaterial) assets. However, the usual practice is to auction these items and place the proceeds in the account. State Unclaimed Property Offices do not hold abandoned real estate. Abandoned real estate is usually sold at auction for back taxes. Questions about abandoned real estate should be addressed to the appropriate county tax office. Please see Chapter Three for more information on the Unclaimed Property Office for each state. Following is a list of assets that may be turned over to state Unclaimed Property Offices.

- account balances due
- checking accounts
- savings accounts
- matured Certificates of Deposit
- security deposits
- unidentified deposits
- uncashed checks
- cashier's checks
- certified checks
- registered checks
- treasurer's checks
- drafts
- warrants
- money orders
- traveler's checks
- foreign exchange checks
- expense checks
- pension checks
- credit checks or memos
- vendor's checks
- outstanding official checks
- Certificate of Deposit interest checks
- mineral proceeds and mineral interests
- net revenue checks
- royalties, overriding royalties
- production payments
- working interest

- bonuses
- delay rentals
- shut-in royalties
- miscellaneous checks and intangible personal property
- wages, payroll, salary
- commissions
- worker's compensation benefits
- payment for goods and services
- customer overpayment
- unidentified remittances
- unrefunded overcharges
- accounts payable
- credit balances
- accounts receivable
- discounts due
- refunds due
- unredeemed gift certificates
- unclaimed loan collateral
- pension and profit share plans
- dissolution or liquidation
- safety deposit box contents
- other tangible property
- unclaimed loan collateral
- court deposits
- escrow funds
- condemnation awards
- missing heir funds
- suspense accounts
- other court deposits
- insurance
- individual policy benefits or claim payments
- group policy benefits or claim payments
- proceeds due beneficiaries
- proceeds from matured policies
- proceeds from endowments and annuities

BARNES & NOBLE# 1988
STORE 1988
8800 TAMPA AVENUE
NORTHRIDGE, CA 91324
(818) 773-0821

REG#03   BOOKSELLER#021
RECEIPT#   28569 07/14/99   11:03 AM

S 1877639400   SECRETS OF FINDING UNCLA
                  1 @ 11.95   11.95

SUBTOTAL   11.95
SALES TAX - 8.25%   .99
TOTAL   12.94
CHECK PAYMENT   12.94

- premium refunds
- unidentified remittances
- other amounts due under policy terms
- agent credit balances
- securities
- dividends
- interest (bond coupons)
- principal payments
- equity payments
- profits
- funds paid to purchase shares
- funds for stocks and bonds
- shares of stock (returned by post office)
- cash for fractional shares
- unexchanged stock of successor corporation
- other certificates of ownership
- underlying shares or other outstanding certificates
- funds for liquidation/redemption of unsurrendered stock or bonds
- debentures
- U.S. government securities
- mutual fund shares
- matured bond principal
- dividend reinvestment plans
- credit balances
- trust, investment and escrow accounts
- paying agents accounts
- undelivered or uncashed dividends
- funds held in fiduciary capacity
- trust vouchers
- pre-need funeral plans
- utility deposits
- membership fees
- refunds and rebates
- capital distributions

How the States Attempt to Locate Rightful Owners

Most states make only half-hearted attempts to locate the rightful owners of unclaimed assets. Methods include advertising in state newspapers, having booths at state fairs, placing lists in public libraries, and using radio and television. Recently, some states have advertised on the Internet and some are installing ATM type machines in shopping malls. Impressive as these methods may seem, they in fact bring in only a small percentage of rightful owners.

Many states also attempt to contact owners through locator services, or companies who specialize in finding people. This method is usually unproductive. In California, for example, they were unable to locate Richard M. Nixon whose home was listed as San Clemente, California. In Texas, one list contained an account for the Treasurer of the United States, Washington, DC. All state lists habitually contain names of prominent individuals and businesses that are listed in the telephone book.

Why do People Abandon Money?

Death is probably the most common reason money and other assets are abandoned. If someone dies without a will or without including everything in their will, that asset may be abandoned and go unclaimed. Other reasons include changes in marital status, job, location, name or retirement.

Also, people simply forget. It's hard for most people to believe, but this is another reason why there is over $40 billion of unclaimed money and assets. For example, people buy traveler's checks for a trip, do not use them, put them aside and forget them. Or people buy stock, move, and fail to send their new address to the transfer agent. Often people establish trust funds for their children and fail or forget to notify the children. These may all eventually become abandoned assets.

People frequently move and fail to fill out a change-of-address card for the Post Office or if a card *is* filled out, the old address information is kept on file for only eighteen months. Correspondence will not be forwarded to the new address after 18 months.

People also fail to notify banks, financial organizations, insurance companies, pension plans, etc., of their change of address. The result is obvious. If the person cannot be located, any money they have due will at some time be turned over to a state Unclaimed Property Office.

Another reason money is abandoned is people rely on others to do things for them. When a family moves, the husband might assume that the wife will take care of notifying everyone of their change of address, and the wife thought she should inform only the bank and utilities. When an elderly parent moves in with an adult child, they may both assume the other notified everyone.

Most people are unaware that an account of theirs has been turned over to the state. Some people believe they can leave money in a bank indefinitely. For example, you go to withdraw money from a savings account that you have not touched in years. You discover that you no longer have a savings account and the cash you thought was earning interest over the years is now in the state Unclaimed Property Office.

Prevention

How can you prevent money and assets from being turned over to the state?

1. Keep bank accounts active by making a deposit or withdrawal occasionally or by having interest posted.

2. Cash all checks that you receive for wages, dividends, insurance premiums and any other money owed to you.

3. Before you move, claim all security deposits. Close bank accounts or have them transferred to your new location. Notify all financial institutions you deal with of your new address. This applies to banks, transfer agents, employers, insurance companies, etc.

4. Fill out a "change-of-address" card at the Post Office whenever you move.

5. Make out a will. This is the best way to make sure your assets end up where you want them after you are gone. Include all pertinent information about all assets and accounts. Tell an attorney or a relative where important records are kept.

How to Find Out who has Unclaimed Money

The Unclaimed Property Office in each state keeps a list of people with unclaimed money and assets. There may be several lists organized by different categories, such as year, type of asset, etc. Chapter Three has the addresses, telephone numbers and information about the assets held by each state Unclaimed Property Office.

The best course of action is to contact the Unclaimed Property Office in all 50 states and the District of Columbia. Some assets could be held by a state even if the individual never lived there. Money held by transfer agents, mutual funds and other financial institutions must be turned over to the state where their home offices are located.

The end of this chapter has sample letters you can use. When listing names on the letters, include any aliases or other names used. Example: Ann Pressley Smith, AKA Mrs. John Paul Smith. In this case, a married name is an alias. Other examples are Harry Holmes Jones, AKA H. H. Jones. In the initial letter, do not include dates of residence or addresses of the claimant. Provide this information only after receiving a claim form from the state Unclaimed Property Office.

For your convenience, the addresses of all 51 Unclaimed Property Offices are set up in Appendix A for you to photocopy and make labels. Using the form letters at the end of this chapter as a guide, type one letter per individual, make 51 photocopies and mail. This is an easy way to contact all states. Repeat this process again each year for a least two years (or based on each state's abandonment period) as some moneys may not yet have been turned over to the Unclaimed Property Office. For example, your aunt died in 1989. The assets she had in bank accounts in some states will be turned over to the Unclaimed Property Offices in 1994, but in other states they will not be turned over until 1996.

How to Claim Money

If you think you might have some money coming to you, here are a few hints to make your search a little easier:
1. Search your basement or attic for any records of inactive bank accounts, unsold stock certificates or other

financial dealings. If you have a claim to make, you will need proof that you are the owner of any abandoned property and that you once lived at the address shown on any old accounts.

2 Contact your state's Unclaimed Property Office to find out if you or a relative is listed as the owner of any abandoned assets. They will assist you in filing a claim to recover it.

3. Check your local newspaper for listings of unclaimed assets or call the paper to find out if and when they plan to publish such listings.

4. If you think that you are owed benefits from any federal or government agency, contact that office directly.

5. If you are approached by an heir searcher, try to locate the assets yourself. Check the probate courts in the counties where your deceased relative lived. You can usually locate inheritances by doing this. If you cannot determine the source of the money, then it is advisable to sign the finders agreement. It is better to receive some money than none at all. Proof of ownership is required to make any claims: drivers license, certified birth certificates, certified death certificates, copies of wills, probate judgments, and other official documents. Each state will tell you exactly what proof of ownership is required before you submit your claim.

Heir Searchers

There is a thriving business in finding people who have abandoned or unclaimed funds. See Part II (Chapters 6-9) for more information.

Sample Letter

Searching for assets for yourself or a living relative.

(Date)

(Address)
(City, State, Zip Code)

Dear Unclaimed Property Office:

Please check your records and let
me know if you have any unclaimed
assets belonging to:

(List names and aliases)

If you have any questions, please
contact me at (work number) or
(home number).

Thank you for your prompt attention
to this matter.

Sincerely,

(Name and signature)

Sample Letter

Searching for assets of a deceased relative.

(Date)

(Address)
(City, State, Zip Code)

Dear Unclaimed Property Office:

Please check your records and let me know if you have any unclaimed assets belonging to:

(list names and aliases)

This person is deceased and I am heir to their estate. If you have any questions, please contact me at (work number) or (home number).

Thank you for your prompt attention to this matter.

Sincerely,

(Name and signature)

Chapter Two

How to obtain money from private businesses and financial institutions

Private businesses and financial institutions include banks, savings and loans, credit unions and insurance companies. These hold millions of dollars of unclaimed money, usually because the owner died, forgot about it or the heir is unaware of the assets. Some examples of assets held by these entities are unclaimed bank accounts, mineral royalties, insurance proceeds and pension plans. For a more detailed listing of these assets, see Chapter One.

These entities will keep these assets for several years before turning them over to the state Unclaimed Property Office. Each state's unclaimed property laws spell out the number of years these assets must be held before relinquishing them to the state. This is known as the "Abandonment Period" and is usually five to seven years.

If you or someone in your family has money held by a private business, you may have the right to claim it. For example: If you owned stock and failed to tell the transfer agent your new address when you moved, you can notify him and obtain possession of this asset. The same is true if a deceased parent owned a mineral right. If you fail to come forward, the assets will, at some time, go to the state Unclaimed Property Office.

It is advisable for you to search the papers of all deceased relatives for any information concerning bank accounts, stocks and bonds, mineral rights, pension plans, etc. Then contact the appropriate business to determine if they have any assets belonging to the deceased. If this is the case and you are the legal heir, you should make a claim.

You will usually have to call the individual company. If you have a question concerning a stock or a life insurance policy and are not sure who to call, the following information should be of help.

Stocks and Bonds

Every year, over 1,500 companies change names and undergo reorganization. This leaves some stockholders believing that their shares are worthless. Millions of dollars of such stocks and bonds are held by corporations and in trust accounts just waiting for people to claim them. Even when companies go bankrupt, there often are funds held in trust for legitimate claimants.

Under most state unclaimed property laws, funds and assets due people who cannot be located are eventually turned over to the state. However, these laws are not always complied with. To determine if an old stock certificate may be valuable, contact Stock Search International. For a small fee, they will research the stock certificate.

Stock Search International
10855 N. Glen Abbey Drive
Tucson, AZ 85737
(800) 537-4523
(520) 544-9395 Fax

Life Insurance Policies

If there is a question about a life insurance policy, you should contact the American Council of Life Insurance. If a deceased relative had a policy that cannot be located and the insurance company's name is not known, the Council may be able to help. Contact them at the address below to receive a form. They will send the completed form to all participating insurance companies. Approximately one hundred of the largest life insurance companies participate in this service. The insurance companies will check their records and contact the designated beneficiary if they find a policy for the name submitted. This process takes from three to six months to complete. You will be notified only if a policy is found. A small fee of $4.50 is charged for each name searched. For more information, contact:

Policy Search
American Council of Life Insurance
1001 Pennsylvania Avenue, NW
Washington, DC 20004
(800) 942-4242

Case Studies

Debbie was talking to her father, Stanford, about investing. He said he had always invested at least 10% of every paycheck in a mutual fund. She asked him where the fund was. He replied that it was with one of the biggest financial companies in the United States but realized that he could not remember the last time he had heard from the company. He thought it had been about four or five years, but he was not particularly worried as it was a large and reputable company. Debbie became concerned. She feared that her father had lost his entire investment, so she contacted the mutual fund. They told Debbie that they had been attempting to locate her father for over six years. The address they had was no longer correct. Debbie provided the current address. The mutual fund mentioned that if Debbie had not contacted them, they would have been required to turn the money over to the state Unclaimed Property Office in six months. The value of Stanford's investment in the mutual fund was worth over $190,000. The money would have taken much longer to locate if Debbie had not questioned her father when she did.

When Marty's father died and the will was probated, he questioned the amount of the estate. Marty felt it should have been larger. He went through all of his father's papers, some of which were over ten years old. He found several receipts and statements concerning a pension plan, but Marty knew his father never received a pension from that firm. He wrote to the company's pension plan office, and they replied that they did have some funds his father had invested. They asked Marty for proof that he was the heir to his father's estate. After he supplied this information, Marty received a check from the pension plan for $43,000. They explained that they had attempted to locate his father, but were unable to find him. His father had moved and failed to give the Post Office a change-of-address card. He had moved to an apartment that was three blocks from his old address and his name was listed in the telephone book, but the pension office had still been unable to find him.

Natalie was taking care of her elderly and widowed mother, Kathrine Mallory. One day while looking at an old photograph album, Natalie found an interesting letter from an insurance company dated "1980." It was about an insurance policy that her mother had taken out on her father. Natalie wrote the company and they replied that Mrs. Mallory had a paid up a policy on her husband with a value of $10,000. They also said they tried to locate Mrs. Mallory for several years without success. They paid the proceeds after Natalie's mother signed a claim form and provided a certified copy of her husband's death certificate.

Kenneth was talking to an old friend about his Army days when he had been stationed at Fort Knox, Kentucky. During the conversation, he recalled that he had a checking account at the bank on the military post. It had been over four years since he left Fort Knox. He began to wonder if he had left some money in the account. He contacted the bank and they did find an account in his name. Kenneth wrote them and asked for the balance of his account. The bank immediately sent him a check for $550. If he had waited much longer, the bank would have been required to send the account to the Kentucky Unclaimed Property Office.

Chapter Three

How to obtain money from state Unclaimed Property Offices

This is a directory of state Unclaimed Property Offices and the regulations of each state.

How to Use This Directory

The legend below explains the categories used in this Directory and their definitions.

(NAME OF STATE)

(*Address and telephone number to contact the state*)

Amount held by state: This is the total value of the assets being held by the state.

Abandonment period: The time period that accounts are held until they are turned over to the state.

Attempts made by state to locate owners: The methods used to locate owners of unclaimed property.

How to make an inquiry: How the state prefers you make inquiries on a name or list of names.

ALABAMA

Alabama Department of Revenue
Unclaimed Property Section
PO Box 327580
Montgomery, AL 36132-7580
(334) 242-9614

Amount held by state: Not available.

Abandonment period: Generally 5 years. Payroll checks are 1 year. Utility deposits are 2 years.

Attempts made by state to locate owners: A notice is published every spring and fall in the county newspapers of the owner's last known address. Dollar amounts are not included in the newspaper.

How to make an inquiry: Alabama requests all inquiries to be made in writing, due to the privacy act. Please include as much information as possible, including a former Alabama address and a Social Security number, if known.

ALASKA

Alaska Department of Revenue
Unclaimed Property Section
PO Box 110420
Juneau, AK 99811-0420
(907) 465-4653
(907) 465-2375 Fax

Amount held by state: Not available.

Abandonment period: Generally 5-7 years for most property.

Attempts made by state to locate owners: Notices in state newspapers. Booths at the state and local fairs. Cross reference names with other state agencies.

How to make an inquiry: By telephone or in writing.

ARIZONA

Arizona Department of Revenue
Unclaimed Property
1600 W. Monroe
Phoenix, AZ 85007-2650
(602) 542-4643
(602) 542-4667 Fax

Amount held by state: $87.3 million.

Abandonment period: Generally 5 years. Money orders are 7 years, utility deposits are 2 years, and traveler's checks are 15 years.

Attempts made by state to locate owners: Notices in state newspapers. Dollar amounts are not included. Match names with Arizona's tax database.

How to make an inquiry: In writing.

ARKANSAS

Auditor of State
Unclaimed Property Division
103 W. Capitol #805
Little Rock, AR 72201
(501) 324-9670
(800) 252-4648
(501) 324-9676 Fax

Amount held by state: $20 million.

Abandonment period: Generally 7 years.

Attempts made by state to locate owners: Notice in state newspapers. Only names with $100 or more are listed. The dollar amounts are not given. Letters are sent to the individual's last known address.

How to make an inquiry: Call or write for a claim form.

CALIFORNIA

Comptroller of the State of California
Division of Collections
Bureau of Unclaimed Property
PO Box 942850
Sacramento, CA 94250-5873
(916) 445-8318
(800) 992-4647 (California only)
(916) 323-2851 Fax

Amount held by state: $1.7 billion.

Abandonment period: Usually 3 years. Traveler's checks are 15 years, money orders are 7 years, cashier's checks are 5 years.

Attempts made by state to locate owners: Notices in state newspapers. Dollar amounts are not given. Letters are sent to the person's last known address. Cross reference with databases of other state agencies.

How to make an inquiry: By telephone or in writing.

COLORADO

Colorado State Treasury
Unclaimed Property Division
1560 Broadway, Suite 1225
Denver, CO 80202
(303) 894-2443
(800) 825-2111
(303) 894-2351 Fax

Amount held by state: $80 million.

Abandonment period: Generally 5 years.

Attempts made by state to locate owners: Notices in the state newspapers. Dollar amounts are not given. Letters are sent to the individual's last known address. Advertisements on radio and television. Booths at public events.

How to make an inquiry: By telephone or in writing.

CONNECTICUT

Unclaimed Property Division
Connecticut State Treasury
PO Box 5665
Hartford, CT 06102
(860) 566-5516
(800) 833-7318
(860) 566-1763 Fax

Amount held by state: $160 million.

Abandonment period: Generally 3–7 years for most property.

Attempts made by state to locate owners: Notices in state newspapers. Dollar amounts are not given. Booths at state fairs. Cross reference information with other state agencies.

How to make an inquiry: By telephone or in writing.

DELAWARE

Delaware State Escheator
PO Box 8931
Wilmington, DE 19899
(302) 577-3397
(302) 577-3106 Fax

Amount held by state: Not available to the public.

Abandonment period: Generally 5 years. Traveler's checks are 15 years.

Attempts made by state to locate owners: Notices in state newspapers. Dollar amounts are not given. Telephone calls are made searching for the correct person. Booths at state fairs. Some matching with other state agency records.

How to make an inquiry: In writing only.

DISTRICT OF COLUMBIA

Officer of the Comptroller
Unclaimed Property Unit
415 12th Street, NW
Room 408
Washington, DC 20004
(202) 727-0063
(202) 727-2389 Fax

Amount held by state: Not available to the public.

Abandonment period: Generally 5-7 years. Traveler's checks are 15 years.

Attempts made by state to locate owners: Notices in state newspapers (twice a year). Letters are sent to the individual's last known address.

How to make an inquiry: You may telephone, but submit in writing if requesting information for more than two names.

FLORIDA

State Comptroller
Abandoned Property Section
State Capitol
Tallahassee, FL 32399-0350
(904) 487-0510
(800) 848-3792 (Florida only)
(904) 922-6014 Fax

Amount held by state: $8.9 million.

Abandonment period: Generally 7 years for most assets.

Attempts made by state to locate owners: Notices in state newspapers twice a year. Dollar amounts are not given.

How to make an inquiry: Request information in writing.

GEORGIA

Department of Revenue
Property Tax Division
Unclaimed Property Section
270 Washington Street, SW
Room 404
Atlanta, GA 30334
(404) 656-4244

Amount held by state: $140 million.

Abandonment period: Generally 5 years; safety deposit box contents held for 2 years; wages and dissolutions 1 year; money orders, 7 years; traveler's checks, 15 years.

Attempts made by state to locate owners: Notices in state newspapers. Dollar amounts are not given.

How to make an inquiry: In writing.

HAWAII

Unclaimed Property Branch
Department of Budget and Finance
PO Box 150
Honolulu, HI 96810
(808) 586-1589

Amount held by state: $37 million.

Abandonment period: Generally 5 years for most items. Stocks are 7 years; payroll is 1 year.

Attempts made by state to locate owners: Notices of individual's names are published twice a year (February and August) in Hawaii newspapers. Only names with $50 or more are listed and dollar amounts are not included.

How to make an inquiry: By telephone or write for information.

IDAHO

Unclaimed Property
State Tax Commission
PO Box 36
Boise, ID 83722
(208) 334-7623

Amount held by state: $18 million.

Abandonment period: Financial institutions are 7 years; any other institution, 5 years; wages and deposits are 1 year.

Attempts made by state to locate owners: A listing of individual's names in state newspapers. Dollar amounts are not given. Advertisements are aired on television stations. Names are cross referenced with Idaho's tax database. "Traveling Locator" attends state and local fairs, malls, and other public places.

How to make an inquiry: By telephone or in writing.

ILLINOIS

Department of Financial Institutions
500 Iles Park Place, Suite 510
Springfield, IL 62718
(217) 782-6692
(217) 785-6999 Fax

Amount held by state: $508 million.

Abandonment period: Five years for most property;
2 years for bankruptcy/liquidations; 15 years for
traveler's checks; 7 years for property held by gov-
ernmental entities.

Attempts made by state to locate owners: Notices of
individual's names are listed in newspapers. Dollar
amounts are not included. Only names with $100 or
more are listed. A list of the names and addresses is
available in libraries. Radio and television promo-
tions. State fairs.

How to make an inquiry: In writing.

INDIANA

Office of Attorney General
Unclaimed Property Division
219 State House
Indianapolis, IN 46204-2794
(317) 232-6348
(800) 447-5598
(317) 232-7979 Fax

Amount held by state: $40 million.

Abandonment period: Generally 7 years for most assets.

Attempts made by state to locate owners: Listing of individual's name and last known address in the state's largest newspapers twice a year. Dollar amounts are not included.

How to make an inquiry: In writing. You may call to request a claim form.

Note: There is a 25 year time restriction to claim funds. After that time the money is put into education.

IOWA

Treasurer of State
Great Iowa Treasure Hunt
Hoover Building
Des Moines, IA 50319
(515) 281-5366
(515) 281-6962 Fax

Amount held by state: $43 million.

Abandonment period: Generally 3 years.

Attempts made by state to locate owners: Names of individuals are published twice a year in the state's largest newspaper. Dollar amounts are not included. Letters are mailed to the individual's last known address. Booths are at state and local fairs or any large gathering. Advertise on radio and television.

How to make an inquiry: By telephone or in writing.

KANSAS

State Treasurer
Unclaimed Property Division
900 SW Jackson, Suite 201
Topeka, KS 66612-1235
(913) 296-4165
(800) 432-0386 (Kansas only)
(913) 296-7950 Fax

Amount held by state: $61 million.

Abandonment period: Generally 5 years; wages are 1 year; traveler's checks are 5 years.

Attempts made by state to locate owners: Listings of names in the county newspapers once a year for accounts of $100 or more. The list is available in Kansas libraries on the Kansas computer terminals. Booths are set up at state and local fairs. Visits are made to each county to search for the rightful owners.

How to make an inquiry: By telephone if you have only a few names to research. For long lists please submit in writing.

KENTUCKY

Kentucky Treasury Department
Capitol Annex, Suite 183
ATTN: Unclaimed Property
Frankfort, KY 40601
(502) 564-4722
(800) 465-4722
(502) 564-7930 Fax

Amount held by state: $30 million.

Abandonment period: Generally 7 years.

Attempts made by state to locate owners: A list of names is published once a year in the state's largest newspapers. Dollar amounts are listed. Letters are mailed to the individual's last know address. Advertise on radio and television stations. Booths at state fairs and conventions.

How to make an inquiry: In writing. You may call to request a claim form.

LOUISIANA

Unclaimed Property Section
Department of Revenue
PO Box 91010
Baton Rouge, LA 70821
(504) 925-7425
(504) 925-3853 Fax

Amount held by state: Not available to the public.

Abandonment period: Generally 5 years; stock and dividends, 7 years; wages and royalties, 2 years; traveler's checks, 15 years.

Attempts made by state to locate owners: A listing of names are published in the state's largest newspapers once a year. Dollar amounts are not included. Letters are mailed to individual's last known address. Advertise on radio and television stations. Special searches are performed in some cases.

How to make an inquiry: Request information in writing.

Note: A list is available for viewing at the office during regular business hours.

MAINE

Abandoned Property Division
Treasury Department
State Office Building
39 State House Street
Augusta, ME 04333-0039
(207) 287-6668
(207) 287-2367 Fax

Amount held by state: $1.7 million.

Abandonment period: Generally 5 years.

Attempts made by state to locate owners: A listing in newspapers. Letters are mailed to the individual's last known address. Booths at state and local fairs. A list is provided to legislators.

How to make an inquiry: By telephone or in writing.

MARYLAND

Comptroller of the Treasury
Unclaimed Property Section
301 W. Preston Street
Baltimore, MD 21201
(410) 225-1700
(800) 782-7383
(410) 333-7150 Fax

Amount held by state: $68 million.

Abandonment period: Generally 5 years.

Attempts made by state to locate owners: A listing
of names in newspapers once a year. Dollar amounts
are not included. Letters are mailed to individual's
last known address. Advertise on radio. Booths at
state fairs and local malls.

How to make an inquiry: By telephone or in writing.

MASSACHUSETTS

Treasury Department
Abandoned Property Division
1 Ash Burton Place, 12th Floor
Boston, MA 02108-1608
(617) 367-3900
(617) 248-3944 Fax

Amount held by state: $400 million.

Abandonment period: Generally 3 years.

Attempts made by state to locate owners: A variety of public service announcements. Listing in the state newspapers twice a year. Dollar amounts are not included. Certified letters to individual's last known address. "Claims Show" booths at state fairs and large public gatherings.

How to make an inquiry: By telephone or in writing.

MICHIGAN

Michigan Department of Treasury
Escheats Division
Abandoned & Unclaimed Property Division
Lansing, MI 48922
(517) 335-4327
(517) 335-4400 Fax

Amount held by state: Not available to the public.

Abandonment period: Most items are 7 years.

Attempts made by state to locate owners: A listing
of names in state newspapers. Dollar amounts are
not included.

How to make an inquiry: By telephone or in writing.

MINNESOTA

Department of Commerce
Unclaimed Property
133 East 7th Street
St. Paul, MN 55101
(612) 296-2568
(800) 925-5668 (Minnesota only)
(612) 296-8591 Fax

Amount held by state: $20 million.

Abandonment period: Generally 3 years. Traveler's checks, 15 years; wages and utility deposits, 1 year. Safety deposit box contents are auctioned every 10 years.

Attempts made by state to locate owners: List names in the state newspapers in April. Only names with $100 or more are listed. Actual dollar amounts are not included. Letters are mailed to the individual's last known address. Booths at the state and local fairs.

How to make an inquiry: If researching a few names you may telephone the office. However, if you are searching for a list of people please request an appointment to view records.

MISSISSIPPI

Unclaimed Property Division
Mississippi Treasury Department
PO Box 138
Jackson, MS 39201
(601) 359-3600
(601) 359-2001 Fax

Amount held by state: Not available to the public.

Abandonment period: 5 years for most property.

Attempts made by state to locate owners: Every three years the state of Mississippi publishes names with amounts of $100 and over. Letters are mailed to individual's last known address.

How to make an inquiry: By telephone or in writing.

MISSOURI

Unclaimed Property Division
PO Box 1004
Jefferson City, MO 65102-1272
(314) 751-0123
(314) 526-6027 Fax

Amount held by state: $80 million.

Abandonment period: Seven years for all property
except traveler's checks (15 years). Court bonds are 1
year and dissolution of business is 2 years.

Attempts made by state to locate owners: Postcards
to individual's last known address. Notices in newspapers. Dollar amounts are not given. List is available in public libraries. Advertise on radio and television. Booths at state and local fairs.

How to make an inquiry: In writing. Be sure to include all information that is known: name, date of
birth, Social Security number, old address. If the Unclaimed Property Office finds a match, they mail a
claim form.

MONTANA

State of Montana
Department of Revenue
Abandoned Property Section
PO Box 5805
Helena, MT 59620
(406) 444-2425
(406) 444-1505 Fax

Amount held by state: Not available to the public.

Abandonment period: Generally 5 years for most items.

Attempts made by state to locate owners: Once a year a listing of names is published in the newspaper. Dollar amounts are not included. Names with $100 and over are published.

How to make an inquiry: You may call if you have only a few names to research. If you have a long list, then request in writing.

NEBRASKA

Office of the State Treasurer
Unclaimed Property Division, Suite 2003
State Capitol
PO Box 94788
Lincoln, NE 68509
(402) 471-3130
(402) 471-4390 Fax

Amount held by state: $30 million.

Abandonment period: Generally 5 years. One year for wages and 15 years for traveler's checks.

Attempts made by state to locate owners: A listing of names with $25 or more of unclaimed money is published once a year in large newspapers. Nebraska has an investigative division that searches for owners. Letters are mailed to individual's last known address.

How to make an inquiry: In writing.

NEVADA

Department of Business/Industry
Unclaimed Property Division
2601 East Sahara Avenue, Suite 270
Las Vegas, NV 89104
(702) 486-4140
(800) 521-0019 (Nevada only)
(702) 486-4177 Fax

Amount held by state: Not available.

Abandonment period: Generally 5 years; pay checks are 1 year; traveler's checks are 15 years.

Attempts made by state to locate owners: Listing in large newspapers of individuals who have $50 or more in the state Unclaimed Property Office. Dollar amounts are not given. Letters are mailed to the individual's last known address. Nevada plans to include state fair functions in the future.

How to make an inquiry: Call or write.

NEW HAMPSHIRE

State Treasury
Division of Abandoned Property
Room 205
State House Annex
Concord, NH 03301
(603) 271-2649
(603) 271-2730 Fax

Amount held by state: Not available.

Abandonment period: Generally 7 years; 1 year for payroll and utility deposits.

Attempts made by state to locate owners: Listing in state newspapers of people who have $25 or more in the state unclaimed property fund. The listing runs in February and August and does not list the dollar amounts. The list is available in state libraries. Letters are mailed to the individual's last known address. Booths at state and local fairs.

How to make an inquiry: Telephone or write.

NEW JERSEY

New Jersey Unclaimed Property
CN 214
Trenton, NJ 08646
(609) 292-9200

Amount held by state: Not available.

Abandonment period: Generally 5 years for most items. Wages are 1 year and traveler's checks are 15 years.

Attempts made by state to locate owners: Listings of names with last known address in county newspapers in February and August of each year. Only individuals who have $50 or more in the unclaimed property account are included.

How to make an inquiry: In writing.

NEW MEXICO

Taxation and Revenue Department
Unclaimed Property Unit
PO Box 25123
Santa Fe, NM 87504-5123
(505) 827-0767
(505) 827-0769
(505) 827-1759 Fax

Amount held by state: $30 million.

Abandonment period: Generally 5 years for most
assets; 15 years for traveler's checks.

Attempts made by state to locate owners: Listing of
names in state newspapers of people who have $25
or more in the state unclaimed property fund. Dollar amounts are not included. Letters are mailed to
individual's last known address.

How to make an inquiry: In writing.

NEW YORK

Office of the State Comptroller
Office of Unclaimed Funds
A.E. Smith Building, 9th Floor
Albany, NY 12236
(518) 474-4038
(800) 221-9311 (New York only)

Amount held by state: $3.4 billion.

Abandonment period: Generally 2-5 years for most
items; traveler's checks are 5 years.

Attempts made by state to locate owners: No list is
published in newspapers. A list is available in public
libraries. Letters are mailed to the individual's last
known address. Booths at state fairs.

How to make an inquiry: Call or request information in writing.

NORTH CAROLINA

Escheat and Unclaimed Property Program
325 N. Salisbury Street
Raleigh, NC 27603-1385
(919) 733-6876
(919) 715-0229 Fax

Amount held by state: $130 million.

Abandonment period: Generally 5 years for most
property.

Attempts made by state to locate owners: Listing in
the Raleigh and Charlotte newspapers. This notice
runs for two weeks usually around September or October. Match names against Department of Revenue
records once a year. Send a list of names to each
county newspaper.

How to make an inquiry: In writing.

NORTH DAKOTA

Unclaimed Property Division
PO Box 5523
Bismarck, ND 58502-5523
(701) 328-2805

Amount held by state: $8 million.

Abandonment period: Generally 3-5 years for most assets.

Attempts made by state to locate owners: Listing in state newspapers of individuals who have $50 or more in the state unclaimed property fund. Dollar amounts are not given. Letters are mailed to the individual's last known address if the dollar amount is large. Booths at state and local fairs. Advertise on radio and television.

How to make an inquiry: In writing.

OHIO

Division of Unclaimed Funds
77 South High Street
20th Floor
Columbus, OH 43266-0545
(614) 466-4433
(614) 752-5078 Fax

Amount held by state: $100 million.

Abandonment period: Generally 5 years for most assets.

Attempts made by state to locate owners: Notices in newspapers listing names of people who have $50 or more in the state unclaimed property account. Ohio has an investigative division to search for the legal owners. Booths at state and county fairs.

How to make an inquiry: In writing.

OKLAHOMA

Oklahoma Tax Commission
Unclaimed Property
2501 Lincoln Blvd
Oklahoma City, OK 73194-0010
(405) 521-4280
(800) 522-8165 (Oklahoma only)
(405) 521-2146 Fax

Amount held by state: $90 million.

Abandonment period: Usually 5 years for most items; payroll/wages are 1 year; traveler's checks are 15 years.

Attempts made by state to locate owners: Notices twice a year in newspaper listing names of people who have $50 or more in the state's unclaimed property fund. Letters are mailed to individual's last known address. Booths at county and state fairs. Advertise on television.

How to make an inquiry: Call or write.

OREGON

Division of State Lands
Unclaimed Property Section
775 Summer Street, NE
Salem, OR 97310
(503) 378-3805

Amount held by state: $40 million.

Abandonment period: Generally 5 years for most items.

Attempts made by state to locate owners: Notices in newspapers listing names of individuals who have $100 or more in the state unclaimed property account. Dollar amounts are not given. Cross reference credit bureau records against unclaimed property list. The state has an investigation division to search for owners of large unclaimed accounts.

How to make an inquiry: No phone inquiries. Submit information in writing.

FEES: Oregon charges a $10 service charge to claim any money valued at $100 or more.

PENNSYLVANIA

State Treasurer
Office of Unclaimed Property
PO Box 1837
Harrisburg, PA 17105-1837
(717) 772-2722
(800) 222-2046 Nationwide
(717) 787-9079 Fax

Amount held by state: $200 million.

Abandonment period: Generally 7 years; traveler's checks 15 years.

Attempts made by state to locate owners: Letters are mailed to the last known address. List names in each county newspaper and the Pennsylvania Bulletin newspaper. Announcements on radio and television. Booths at state fairs and malls.

How to make an inquiry: Call or write.

RHODE ISLAND

Unclaimed Property Division
PO Box 1435
Providence, RI 02901-1435
(401) 277-6505
(401) 274-3865 Fax

Amount held by state: $45 million.

Abandonment period: Generally 3 years.

Attempts made by state to locate owners: Yearly lists in state newspapers of people who have $50 or more in the unclaimed property account. Dollar amounts are not given. The list is also available in public libraries. A staff locator searches for the owners of the larger unclaimed accounts. Names are listed on cable television. Booths at state and county fairs and at some malls.

How to make an inquiry: Telephone or write.

SOUTH CAROLINA

South Carolina Department of Revenue
Abandoned Property Division
PO Box 125
Columbia, SC 29214
(803) 737-4771

Amount held by state: $50 million.

Abandonment period: Generally 5 years for most property. Payroll and utility deposits are 1 year.

Attempts made by state to locate owners: Notices in state newspapers listing names of people who have $50 or more in the unclaimed property fund. Dollar amounts are not given. The state checks their records against state tax records for current address. Letters are mailed to the individual's last known address. Booths at state and county fairs and malls.

How to make an inquiry: Please call or write.

SOUTH DAKOTA

Unclaimed Property Division
State Treasury
500 East Capitol Avenue
Pierre, SD 57501-5070
(605) 773-3378
(605) 773-3115 Fax

Amount held by state: $7 million.

Abandonment period: Generally 5 years. Traveler's checks are 15 years.

Attempts made by state to locate owners: Notices are run in state newspapers every February and September listing the names of people who have $50 or more in the unclaimed property account. Dollar amounts are not given. Booths at state fairs and malls.

How to make an inquiry: By telephone or in writing.

TENNESSEE

State of Tennessee
Treasury Department
Unclaimed Property Division
A. Jackson Office Bldg, 9th Floor
Nashville, TN 37243-0242
(615) 741-6499

Amount held by state: $60 million.

Abandonment period: Generally 5 years for most property.

Attempts made by state to locate owners: Listing in state newspapers of people who have $50 or more in the state unclaimed property account. Dollar amounts are not given. Match other state records against the names. Letters are mailed to individual's last known address. Attend state fairs.

How to make an inquiry: In writing.

TEXAS

Texas Treasury
Unclaimed Property Division
PO Box 12019
Austin, TX 78711-2019
(512) 463-6060
(800) 321-2274 (Texas only)

Amount held by state: $400-500 million.

Abandonment period: Generally 3 years for most property.

Attempts made by state to locate owners: Notices in state newspapers of people who have $50 or more in the unclaimed property account. Dollar amounts are not given. The list is available in public libraries. Texas has a staff locator. Letters are mailed to individual's last known address. Attend state fairs. Promotions for radio. Texas has over 50 kiosk machines available in malls that allow people to access the unclaimed property information.

How to make an inquiry: Call or write.

FEES: For amounts of $100-5,000 handling fee is 1% of total. For amounts of $5,000 and over, handling fee is 1.5% of total. Fees will be deducted at time of payment.

UTAH

Unclaimed Property Division
Treasurer, State of Utah
341 South Main, 5th Floor
Salt Lake City, UT 84111
(801) 533-4101
(801) 533-4096 Fax

Amount held by state: $25 million.

Abandonment period: Generally 5 years for most property.

Attempts made by state to locate owners: Notices once a year in state newspapers of people who have $50 or more in the unclaimed property account. Attend state fairs.

How to make an inquiry: In writing.

VERMONT

State Treasurer
Abandoned Property Division
133 State Street, 2nd Floor
Montpelier, VT 05633-6200
(802) 828-2407
(802) 828-2772 Fax

Amount held by state: $3 million.

Attempts made by state to locate owners: Notices in state newspapers every October listing names of people who have $50 or more of unclaimed property. Dollar amounts are not included. List will soon be available in libraries. Attend state fairs. Letters are mailed to individual's last known address if the amount is $25 or more.

How to make an inquiry: Please call or write to request a form. If searching more than two names, please submit in writing.

VIRGINIA

Commonwealth of Virginia
Division of Treasury
PO Box 2478
Richmond, VA 23207-2478
(804) 225-2393
(800) 468-1088 (Virginia only)
(804) 786-4653 Fax

Amount held by state: Not available to the public.

Abandonment period: Generally 5 years. Payroll is 1 year.

Attempts made by state to locate owners: Notices in state newspapers listing names of people who have money in the unclaimed property account. Dollar amounts are not given. Other searches are conducted using automated databases. The state has an investigative division. Attend state and local fairs.

How to make an inquiry: If asking about one or two names, you may telephone. Please write if requesting information for a large number of names.

WASHINGTON

Department of Revenue
Special Programs Division
Unclaimed Property Section
PO Box 448
Olympia, WA 98507
(360) 586-2736
(800) 435-2429 (Washington, Oregon, Idaho only)
(360) 586-2163 Fax

Amount held by state: $100 million.

Abandonment period: Generally 5 years for most assets. Paychecks and utility deposits are 1 year. Traveler's checks are 15 years.

Attempts made by state to locate owners: Notices twice a year in 39 county newspapers listing names of people who have $75 or more in an unclaimed property account. The state has a full-time locator. Washington Information System is available statewide on machines similar to ATMs.

How to make an inquiry: Call or write.

WEST VIRGINIA

State Treasurer's Office
Division of Unclaimed Property
Bldg 1, Rm E145
1900 Kanawha Blvd, East
Charleston, WV 25305
(304) 343-4000
(800) 422-7498
(304) 346-6602 Fax

Amount held by state: $12 million.

Abandonment period: Five years for non-interest bearing accounts; 15 years for interest bearing accounts.

Attempts made by state to locate owners: Once a year a list of people who have $50 or more of unclaimed money appears in state newspapers. Dollar amounts are not listed. Staff field personnel search for owners. Letters are mailed to individual's last known address. Promotions are run on television.

How to make an inquiry: In writing.

WISCONSIN

State Treasurer's Office
Unclaimed Property Division
PO Box 2114
Madison, WI 53701-2114
(608) 267-7977
(608) 261-6799 Fax

Amount held by state: $50 million.

Abandonment period: Generally 5 years for most items; 15 years for traveler's checks.

Attempts made by state to locate owners: Once every two years a list of people who have $50 or more in the unclaimed property account appears in each county newspaper. Dollar amounts are not given. The list is available in public libraries. Attend state and county fairs.

How to make an inquiry: In writing.

WYOMING

Wyoming Unclaimed Property
122 West 25th Street
1st Floor West
Herschler Building
Cheyenne, WY 82002
(307) 777-5590

Amount held by state: $5.4 million.

Abandonment period: General rule is 5 years.

Attempts made by state to locate owners: A notice is published each March in state newspapers listing the people who have $50 or more in the state unclaimed property account. Dollar amounts are not given. An information brochure is available at libraries. Booths at the state fair.

How to make an inquiry: By telephone or in writing.

Case Studies

Mickey lived in Minnesota until she became too old to care for herself. She then moved to Florida, where she lived with her sister until her death in 1982. At the suggestion of a nephew, Mickey's sister checked with the Unclaimed Property Office of Minnesota who informed her that they had two accounts in Mickey's name worth over $6,000. After submitting the requested information to Minnesota, the sister received this money within a few weeks.

Jake retired in 1975 and lived on his Social Security check. Jake's son thought his father had money in retirement funds where he was formerly employed. A telephone call to the Unclaimed Property Office in the state where his father worked proved him right. Over $15,000 in pension funds had been sent to the office by his former employers. They had been unable to contact Jake, even though he had lived at the same address for 20 years.

Ashley was a family genealogist. One day she made a list of her immediate relatives (grandparents, mother, father and cousins), and wrote all the state Unclaimed Property Offices to determine if they had any unclaimed money for these family members. To her surprise, six accounts were located in six states for different members of her family. These accounts varied in value from $50 to $450. This was a very good return for an investment of only $16 in stamps. Ashley now plans to write all state Unclaimed Property Offices again next year because more money may be turned over to them in the future.

Mike and his sister, Yvonne, knew that their aunt who died in 1970 had a great deal of money. The aunt's will had been probated, but the estate was worth only about $10,000. They decided to write to the Unclaimed Property Offices in the five states where their aunt had lived. They located two accounts, each worth over $100,000. This money had been turned over to the states, because their aunt had moved and had forgotten to submit a change-of-address card to the Post Office.

Chapter Four

How to obtain money
through probate courts

Probate courts are state courts and there is usually one in each county. These are the courts that oversee the distribution of a person's assets when they die.

If a person dies with a will (testate) the court insures that the assets are given to the heirs designated in the person's will. This is normally not a problem. However, if the court cannot locate any of the designated heirs, then the court can have a search made. However, few probate courts have the facilities to do such searches. These are usually done by private investigators and probate researchers hired by the administrator of the will. If the search is unsuccessful the settlement may be delayed or after a designated period, the money for the missing heirs will be sent to the state Unclaimed Property Office. If the court is unaware of assets owned by the deceased that were not mentioned in the will, then these assets will ultimately go to the state Unclaimed Property Office.

If the decedent dies without a will (intestate) the estate is given to the individuals designated by the appropriate state law. If these designated heirs can be located then the estate is disbursed. But if they cannot be located, the estate is held by the court and may at some time be sent to the state Unclaimed Property Office.

If you believe someone in your family who has died may have had some money that was not disbursed, you should do the following:

1. Determine the date and place of death.
2. Contact the probate court in the county where the relative resided.
3. Ask the court the status of the probate.
4. If the case is still open, contact the administrator of the estate. Find out if there was a will and if there were designated heirs.
5. If the decedent died without a will, find out who in your family can legally inherit the estate.

If the heirs cannot be located, find out if the estate has been turned over to the state Unclaimed Property Office. If so, contact that office and request the necessary forms to claim the estate. Return this claim with the necessary documents to prove your relationship to the deceased.

An important point to keep in mind in cases like this: Mothers and fathers can inherit as well as brothers, sisters, children, aunts, uncles and first cousins. In a few states, second cousins can inherit. All relatives must be related by blood and not by marriage. Laws concerning inheritance by adopted children varies from state to state.

The Sourcebook of County Court Records by BRB Publications is an excellent resource. It lists the addresses and telephone numbers of the repositories of probate court records in the 50 states.

Case Studies

Phyllis' Aunt Avis died in 1983. Phyllis's mother told her on several occasions that Avis was going to leave Phyllis some money when she died; however, she never received anything. One day Phyllis decided to contact the probate court near where Aunt Avis had lived. It was discovered that the case had not been closed. In her will, Avis left the bulk of her estate to a college, but she had also willed $20,000 to Phyllis. The administrator of the estate had tried but was unable to locate Phyllis because she had married shortly before her aunt had died. The administrator did not know her married name nor her new address. The money was given to Phyllis after she provided a certified copy of her birth certificate, her mother's birth certificate and a certified copy of her marriage license.

Jonathan was adopted when he was three years old. His adopted father died in 1990. In his will, he gave all his estate to his natural son, Kevin who was killed in an automobile accident a few days before his father died. Kevin had been married but did not have any children. Jonathan knew about the terms of his adopted father's will. He was told that under the circumstances, he would not get anything. Last year, he was talking to an attorney on another matter and the subject of the will came up. The attorney told him that the information he had received was incorrect. As the only surviving heir, he was entitled to the entire estate. Jonathan checked with the probate court and was told to provide a certified copy of his birth certificate and a copy of his drivers license. The judge ruled that Jonathan was the sole heir to an estate worth over $100,000.

Steve had an Uncle Dave who died a few years ago. Uncle Dave had never married, had no children, and owned a prosperous business. Steve's mother said that Uncle Dave had nothing to do with her or any other member of their family for over twenty years. Steve was curious as to what happened to his uncle's estate. He called the probate court near where his uncle lived and discovered that the entire estate was about to be transferred to the state Unclaimed Property Office. The administrator had no information of any living relatives and was about to recommended that the case be closed. However, Steve's inquiry resulted in Steve's mother receiving the entire estate, since she was the next of kin.

Carl was taking care of his elderly father, Derek, who often spoke of his younger brother. The family last heard from him five years ago, so Carl attempted to contact his uncle. He found out that he had died about three years ago and obtained a copy of his obituary. It showed that he had no relatives and that he was buried in a National Cemetery. Carl contacted the probate court in the county where his uncle had lived. The court had his estate of $75,000. They had been unable to find any heirs. Carl produced the information and Derek received the entire estate as next of kin.

Chapter Five

How to obtain money from the federal government

There are many federal government agencies that are holding billions of dollars in unclaimed assets. These agencies include the Social Security Administration, Internal Revenue Service, Federal Housing Administration, United States Treasury, Office of Personnel Management, Department of Veterans Affairs and the Armed Forces.

Some assets have been abandoned by the rightful owner and others have never been claimed for various reasons. Each agency has different types of assets. The following information will help you determine if you or your family has money due. Remember that the federal government is not subject to state unclaimed property laws (escheat laws).

Social Security Administration

The Social Security Administration administers three programs that millions of people are eligible but few ever apply for. They are the Social Security disability program, Supplemental Security Income (SSI) program and regular old age Social Security insurance. The main reason why people do not claim or apply for these benefits is that they are unaware of the program and/or they believe the Social Security Administration will automatically notify them if they are eligible.

Regular old age Social Security benefits can be paid to a retired worker and spouse as early as age 62. But millions of people are unaware of this fact and think they must wait until they are 65 years of age. Payments in this program can be as high as $1,800 per month.

The Social Security disability program provides for qualified covered individuals at any age. A person who is less than 65 years old must be totally disabled or unable to do substantial work to be considered eligible for this program. This program pays a monthly payment up to $1,800 and provides medical insurance.

Supplemental Security Income (SSI) provides for permanently disabled people who have low incomes and generally are not entitled to the Social Security disability program. Monthly payments and medical coverage are provided under this program.

If you or someone you know may qualify to receive Social Security benefits or if you have any questions, call your local Social Security Administration office or call toll free, (800) 772-1213.

Note: The Social Security Administration is currently holding $75 million in uncashed benefit checks. They will replace any missing check. Please contact Social Security, (800) 772-1213.

Internal Revenue Service

The Internal Revenue Service does not keep a national list of uncashed tax refund checks and their owners. Each Internal Revenue Service district maintains its own list. Once a year, in late September or October, the district offices publish the names of people who have not cashed their refund checks.

Note: Forbes magazine reported that the National Taxpayers Union discovered through a Freedom of Information Act inquiry that their was $25 million of uncashed tax refund checks for the years 1985–1987. The average check was for $425.

To obtain information about a check or make a claim, contact your local IRS office and request form 3911, "Taxpayers Statement Regarding Refund."

United States Treasury Department

The treasury's U.S. Savings Bond Division is holding billions of dollars in matured, non-interest bearing debt securities. They report that $1.33 billion in bonds issued before 1948 have not been redeemed by their owners. Request form PD 1048 to have a lost, stolen, or mutilated bond replaced. The individual's name and Social Security number is required for a bond search. Contact:

Bureau of the Public Debt
PO Box 1328
Parkersburg, WV 26106-1328
(304) 480-6112

Federal Housing Administration

The Federal Housing Administration (FHA) is holding over $65 million in mortgage insurance refunds. This money is due to borrowers who have paid FHA home loans early or defaulted. For information, contact:

Distributive Shares Branch
Department of HUD
PO Box 23699
Washington, DC 20036
(703) 235-8117
Note: Please have FHA number available.

Office of Personnel Management

The Office of Personnel Management, which handles the payroll for all civil service employees, holds paychecks and benefit checks for federal employees and their heirs. This office also handles reports of death. They are able to research and verify that the deceased individual received all pay or benefits, and if they had a life insurance policy. Contact:

Office of Personnel Management
Room 1323B
1900 E. Street, NW
Washington, DC 20415
(202) 606-0500

Department of Veterans Affairs

The Department of Veterans Affairs (VA), formerly the Veterans Administration, issues checks for many different programs. These programs include disability compensation and education benefits checks to eligible veterans and their dependents. Any checks not cashed by the beneficiary within one year of issuance will be void. If the VA and the beneficiary can verify that the check is lost or stolen, the VA office can issue payment to the veteran or eligible dependent. Proper identification from the beneficiary is necessary to make any claims. The Department of Veterans Affairs' toll free number is (800) 827-1000. This number will connect you with your local VA Regional Office or you may write your local office.

Millions of veterans of the armed forces are entitled to numerous benefits and compensation that they are eligible for from the VA. Veterans do not apply for these benefits simply because they do not think they are eligible or they erroneously believe that the VA will contact them automatically if they are eligible. All benefits provided by the VA must be applied for by the veteran or his dependents.

Disability compensation payments are as much as $1,500 a month. A service connected disability can be paid for occurrences that happened over fifty years ago. There is no time limit when a veteran may apply for disability benefits. The VA has a pension program for eligible veterans, home loans, life insurance and college education assistance. Another benefit provided to veterans and their spouses is a burial allowance and free interment in VA National Cemeteries. The veteran or next of kin must apply for benefits. If you think you may be eligible, contact any VA Regional Office or call (800) 827-1000.

Following are the addresses of the VA Regional Offices:

ALABAMA
VA Regional Office
345 Perry Hill Road
Montgomery, AL 36109

ALASKA
VA Regional Office
2925 Debarr Road
Anchorage, AK 99508

ARIZONA
VA Regional Office
3225 N Central Avenue
Phoenix, AZ 85012

ARKANSAS
VA Regional Office
Bldg 65 Ft. Roots
N.Little Rock, AR 72115

CALIFORNIA
VA Regional Office
11000 Wilshire Blvd
Los Angeles, CA 90024

CALIFORNIA
VA Regional Office
2022 Camino Del Rio N.
San Diego, CA 92108

CALIFORNIA
VA Regional Office
1301 Clay Street
Oakland, CA 94612

COLORADO
VA Regional Office
44 Union Blvd.
Denver, CO 80225

CONNECTICUT
VA Regional Office
450 Main Street
Hartford, CT 06103

DELAWARE
VA Regional Office
1601 Kirkwood Hwy
Wilmington, DE 19805

DISTRICT OF COLUMBIA
VA Regional Office
1120 Vermont Avenue, NW
Washington, DC 20421

FLORIDA
VA Regional Office
144 1st Avenue, South
St Petersburg, FL 33701

GEORGIA
VA Regional Office
730 Peachtree Street. NE
Atlanta, GA 30365

HAWAII
VA Regional Office
300 Ala Moana Blvd
Honolulu, HI 96850

IDAHO
VA Regional Office
805 W. Franklin Street
Boise, ID 83702

ILLINOIS
VA Regional Office
536 S. Clark Street
Chicago, IL 60680

INDIANA
VA Regional Office
575 N. Pennsylvania Street
Indianapolis, IN 46202

IOWA
VA Regional Office
210 Walnut Street
Des Moines, IA 50309

KANSAS
VA Regional Office
5500 E. Kellogg
Wichita, KS 67218

KENTUCKY
VA Regional Office
545 S. Third Street
Louisville, KY 40202

LOUISIANA
VA Regional Office
701 Loyola Avenue
New Orleans, LA 70113

MAINE
VA Regional Office
Route 17 East
Togus, ME 04330

MARYLAND
VA Regional Office
31 Hopkins Plaza
Baltimore, MD 21201

MASSACHUSETTS
VA Regional Office
JFK Fed Bldg Gov Cen
Boston, MA 02203

MICHIGAN
VA Regional Office
477 Michigan Avenue
Detroit, MI 48226

MINNESOTA
VA Regional Office
Fed Bldg Ft Snelling
St Paul, MN 55111

MISSISSIPPI
VA Regional Office
100 W. Capitol Street
Jackson, MS 39269

MISSOURI
VA Regional Office
400 South 18th Street
St Louis, MO 63103

MONTANA
VA Regional Office
Williams St & Hwy 12W
Ft Harrison, MT 59636

NEBRASKA
VA Regional Office
5631 S. 48th Street
Lincoln, NE 68516

NEVADA
VA Regional Office
1201 Terminal Way
Reno, NV 89520

NEW HAMPSHIRE
VA Regional Office
275 Chestnut Street
Manchester, NH 03101

NEW JERSEY
VA Regional Office
20 Washington Place
Newark, NJ 07102

NEW MEXICO
VA Regional Office
500 Gold Avenue, SW
Albuquerque, NM 87102

NEW YORK
VA Regional Office
111 W. Huron Street
Buffalo, NY 14202

NEW YORK
VA Regional Office
245 W. Houston Street
New York, NY 10014

NORTH CAROLINA
VA Regional Office
251 N. Main Street
Winston-Salem, NC 27155

NORTH DAKOTA
VA Regional Office
2101 Elm Street
Fargo, ND 58102

OHIO
VA Regional Office
1240 E. 9th Street
Cleveland, OH 44199

OKLAHOMA
VA Regional Office
125 S. Main Street
Muskogee, OK 74401

OREGON
VA Regional Office
1220 SW 3rd Avenue
Portland, OR 97204

PENNSYLVANIA
VA Regional Office
1000 Liberty Avenue
Pittsburgh, PA 15222

PUERTO RICO
VA Regional Office
GPO Box 4867
San Juan, PR 00936

SOUTH CAROLINA
VA Regional Office
1801 Assembly Street
Columbia, SC 29201

TENNESSEE
VA Regional Office
110 9th Avenue South
Nashville, TN 37203

TEXAS
VA Regional Office
1400 N. Valley Mills Drive
Waco, TX 76799

VERMONT
VA Regional Office
N. Hartland Road
White River Jnct, VT 05001

PENNSYLVANIA
VA Regional Office
PO Box 8079
Philadelphia, PA 19101

PHILIPPINES
VA Regional Office
1131 Roxas Blvd.
APO AP 96440

RHODE ISLAND
VA Regional Office
380 Westminster Mall
Providence, RI 02903

SOUTH DAKOTA
VA Regional Office
2501 W. 22nd Street
Sioux Falls, SD 57117

TEXAS
VA Regional Office
6900 Almedia Road
Houston, TX 77030

UTAH
VA Regional Office
125 S. State Street
Salt Lake City, UT 84147

VIRGINIA
VA Regional Office
210 Franklin Rd. SW
Roanoke, VA 24011

WASHINGTON
VA Regional Office
915 2nd Avenue
Seattle, WA 98174

WEST VIRGINIA
VA Regional Office
640 4th Avenue
Huntington, WV 25701

WISCONSIN
VA Regional Office
5000 W National Ave
Milwaukee, WI 53295

WYOMING
VA Regional Office
2360 E Pershing Blvd
Cheyenne, WY 82001

A deceased veteran may have had a VA Life Insurance policy. If the VA has not been notified of a veteran's death, they will not take any action to find or pay the beneficiaries of the policy. Contact the Veterans Affairs' Life Insurance Office to inquire if a deceased veteran had a life insurance policy. If the veteran separated or retired from the military over five years ago, contact:

Veterans Affairs Insurance
PO Box 8079
Philadelphia, PA 19101
(800) 669-8477

If the veteran separated or retired from the military fewer than five years ago, contact:

Servicemen Group Life Insurance
213 Washington Street
Newark, NJ 07102
(800) 419-1473
(201) 802-7676 (from overseas call collect)

Armed Forces Reserve Component

Thousands of people who have 20 or more years of service in the reserve components of the armed forces have millions of dollars of unclaimed retirement pay.

Former members of the Army, Navy, Air Force, Marine Corps, and Coast Guard reserves may be unaware that they are eligible for monthly retired pay. They either do not know they are eligible or believe the military will start sending monthly checks automatically when they become eligible. However, the laws require that individuals must apply for their military benefits. For further information, contact the appropriate branch of the armed forces:

> Army Reserve and Army National Guard
> Army Reserve Personnel Center
> ATTN: Retired Affairs
> 9700 Page Blvd
> St. Louis, MO 63132-5100

> Navy Reserve
> Navy Reserve Personnel Command
> ATTN: Retired Affairs
> New Orleans, LA 70146-5000

> Air Force and Air National Guard
> Air Force Reserve Personnel Center
> ATTN: Retired Affairs
> Denver, CO 80280-5000

> Marine Corps Reserve
> Marine Corps Reserve Support Center
> ATTN: Retired Affairs
> 10950 El Monte
> Overland Park, KS 66211-1408

Coast Guard Reserve
US Coast Guard
ATTN: Reserve Retired Affairs
2100 2nd Street, SW
Washington, DC 20593-0001

Case Studies

Charles was a veteran who died in 1989. He had a will that listed his two sons as sole heirs. The will was probated and the two sons received their inheritance. One of the sons thought that since his father had been in the military, he might have had an insurance policy with the Department of Veterans Affairs. A call to the VA Insurance Office in Philadelphia confirmed his suspicions. The two sons received over $30,000 from this insurance policy.

Joseph had just graduated from high school and was talking to an Army recruiter. He explained to Joseph the benefits of joining the Army reserve. One of the benefits was that he could begin receiving retired pay and benefits after twenty years of reserve service. Joseph knew that his father, who had Alzheimer's disease, had been in the reserve for over twenty years but was not receiving any pay or benefits from the Army. He wrote to the Army Reserve Personnel Center in St. Louis, MO. They told him that his father was indeed entitled to retired pay and other benefits. They sent the necessary forms which Joseph completed and had his father sign. His father now receives a monthly check for $450. He is also entitled to use the military hospital, exchange and commissary.

Pam was talking to her elderly mother, Marla, who told Pam that she had purchased many U.S. Savings bonds while she was working. Marla said that she had never cashed them and could not remember what she did with them. A search of the house, safe deposit box and a family safe failed to produce the bonds. Pam wrote to the federal government to get the bonds replaced. Marla knew that she had paid for the bonds by payroll deduction. The government determined that she did in fact have over $15,000 in bonds that had never been redeemed. With the proof of payment from her paychecks, the government replaced the bonds.

Todd and Mandy purchased a home in 1984. They obtained an FHA insured loan. In 1992, they sold their home and moved to another city. They read an article in the newspaper that people who had FHA loans may have an insurance refund due to them. They wrote to the FHA, who sent them a form to fill out. They returned the form and two months later received a check for $87.

Robert was 72 years old and lived by himself since his wife passed away. It had become extremely difficult for Robert to take care of himself, so in 1991 he moved to another town and lived with his daughter. Immediately after Robert moved, his daughter contacted the Social Security office and gave them her father's new address. In 1995, Robert's son was visiting with his sister and they were discussing their father's income. He asked his sister how much Robert was receiving from the Department of Veterans Affairs. She said she did not know anything about money from the VA. So the son called the VA and they told him that they had several checks totaling over $5,000 which had been returned by the Post Office. No one had given the Post Office a change-of-address card for Robert. The VA corrected their records and sent the checks. Robert now receives his regular monthly check from the VA.

Christine Bryant worked for the federal government as a civil service employee for 40 years. When she died last year in Florida, her estate was worth $45,000. This went to her younger sister, Tari, who was her only living relative. Tari thought that her sister may have had an insurance policy with the federal government so she wrote to the Office of Personnel Management. They did have a policy for $30,000 but had been unable to locate Tari, who was listed as beneficiary on Christine's policy. The address they had was where Tari lived over ten years ago. After a claim form was completed, Tari received the $30,000.

Spencer was a very conscientious person. He always mailed in his federal income tax in January of every year and always received a tax refund, usually around $300. Last year, he moved a few weeks after he mailed his income tax form. He filled out a change-of-address form and gave it to his postman. After he moved, he decided to join the Coast Guard and he sent in another change-of-address card. After finishing boot camp, he was sent to two different schools and later was assigned to a Coast Guard base in Alaska. Spencer knew he had not reported all his change of addresses to the Post Office. He assumed that since he was in the military, he could be located easily. He was wrong. The following year he thought about his refund and he wrote to the IRS. They were holding a refund check for him in the amount of $297. They sent it to him immediately. Spencer has learned his lesson and always prepares a change-of-address card whenever he moves.

Part II

Professional
Heir Searching

Chapter Six

Heir searching as a profession

It is obvious after reading the first part of this book that there are billions of dollars of money that rightful owners are unaware of. It is also obvious that the government, or whoever happens to be holding the money, will never notify the majority of the owners. Additionally, few of the rightful owners will find out or claim this money. Therefore, it is evident that there are many opportunities to collect *finder's fees* for locating the right owners.

> **Finder's Fee:** Legal compensation for professional services paid to an individual or organization to locate an asset that is unknown to the rightful owner or heir.

An heir searcher is an individual who brings together unclaimed money or inheritances and the rightful owners or heirs. He normally receives a finder's fee. This is usually achieved with an agreement signed by the heir or owner.

> **Heir Searcher:** An individual or a company who finds unclaimed money, then locates and notifies the rightful owner or heir for a fee.

> **Heir:** A person who receives or has the right to receive someone's estate after that person dies.

> **Inheritance:** The estate transferred to an heir.

Heir searching can be a full- or part-time occupation. The amount of money to be made depends entirely upon the enterprise of the searcher. A good searcher can easily make $100,000 or more every year. Many do.

Other names for an heir searcher are heir tracer, probate researcher, searcher, and genealogical researcher. Just as in the first part of the book, unclaimed money can mean unclaimed inheritances, forgotten bank accounts, etc. Being an heir searcher does not mean that you are only looking for the heir to an inheritance. It can also mean contacting people who are alive and the rightful owners of unclaimed money.

Once you locate the rightful owner, you will find out that not everyone is willing to pay a finder's fee. Many will want all of the money and will try to locate the money themselves (few will be successful). Some people cannot be convinced that they are entitled to any money. Others may think you are running a scam. So be aware that not everyone will be willing to sign a contract which allows for a finder's fee, but most will.

Individuals with experience in research related activities often become heir searchers. Examples are genealogical researchers, probate researchers, private investigators, courthouse researchers and librarians.

Most heir searchers start on a part-time basis and derive the majority of their income from other occupations.

Complications

Heir searching is not necessarily as easy as it sounds. Some cases can get very complicated. For example when there is more than one heir, some may be difficult to determine and locate. This is particularly true in cases involving an individual who has been married more than once and has children by both marriages.

Additionally, some people do not want to be found. They may be delinquent on child support, wanted by the law or avoiding creditors. Often people have had a falling out with other members of their family and do not wish any contact with them, no matter how beneficial the reason. Others may have mental problems or have had "bad experiences" with friends and relatives and want little or no contact with "strangers."

It is hard to believe, but there are many people who have reasons they abandoned money in the first place. They are aware that money is due to them, but want no part of it. A very good example of this is people who have had bad marriages that ended in divorce and do not want any assets that remind them or relate to the marriage. Other people have "disowned" their parents and simply refuse to take any money, inheritances or gifts from them. They cannot believe that the money has "no strings attached." Some people refuse money because they will have to pay more taxes or they may have to give up some benefit, such as a VA pension or welfare.

Some people will not believe they have money coming even if you do find them. This occurs frequently. People often state that they were from a very poor family and the family accounted for every penny they ever owned. Others state that, because of their ethnic background, it is impossible for anyone in their family to have any unclaimed money at all. There are also many people suffering from mental illnesses who cannot fully understand that they are due an inheritance, trust or abandoned money. Many of these are street people.

Finder's Fee

The profit of being an heir searcher is in the finder's fee. The average finder's fee is one third (33.3%) of the estate. Some states restrict the amount of the finder's fee to 10, 20 or 30 percent (see Chapter Seven). When not restricted by state law, the normal fee requested is 40% for small accounts ($15,000 to $25,000) and 33.3% for accounts larger than that. Fees are negotiable, particularly when the rightful owner is contacted by more than one heir searcher (see "Competition," later in this chapter).

> **Estate:** All the property, real or
> personal, owned by an individual.

Unless you do all the work yourself, you will not receive all of the finder's fee. In the following example, I found the rightful heir to an estate worth $300,000 and the finder's fee was 33.3%. The reporter who notified me of the estate received 5% of the total estate. The attorney who handled the probate issues for me received 10% of the total estate, their portion is paid out of the finder's fee. My miscellaneous costs included long distance telephone calls, postage and computer searches.

Total amount of estate	$300,000
Finder's fee	-100,000
Amount heir received	$200,000
Attorney's fee	30,000
Reporter's fee	15,000
Miscellaneous costs	500
Total expenses	$45,500
Finder's fee	$100,000
Total expenses	-45,500
My total earnings	$ 54,500

All three expenses were paid out of the $100,000 finder's fee. However much is left over, in this case $54,500, which is my heir searcher's fee. It just so happens that in this case my "cut" of the pie is about 18% of the total estate.

If this were not a probate matter, an attorney would not have been necessary. If I found the case myself, there would be no reporter's fee. Therefore, I would receive all of the finder's fee, less my expenses.

Where to Find Unclaimed and Abandoned Money

The first part of this book detailed the types and locations of unclaimed money. These will now be discussed in connection with heir searching:

1. Private businesses and financial organizations, trust funds, mutual funds, transfer agents, etc.
2. State Unclaimed Property Offices
3. Probate courts
4. Federal agencies

Some private businesses, such as insurance companies, have a great deal of money available in unclaimed pension funds and financial accounts. Often, heir searchers can reach an agreement with these companies to locate the owners of the accounts. These agreements allow the heir searcher to receive a specified percentage of the unclaimed account (from the owner) once the owner has been located. This finder's fee is normally between 20 and 40 percent. These financial institutions would prefer that the rightful owner, or heir, obtain the money rather than having to turn it over to the state. This is to insure the goodwill of current and future customers.

All of the state Unclaimed Property Offices (UPOs) are listed in Chapter Three. These offices maintain a *list of accounts*.

List of Accounts: The names of individuals
who own assets that are currently held by a state
Unclaimed Property Office. This list sometimes
includes last known addresses and dollar amounts.

These lists are maintained in various forms such as computer, hard copy (paper) or microfilm, and are updated periodically. Most states sell this list to heir searchers. Some will only sell to licensed private investigators. Other states have lists available in public libraries, the Unclaimed Property Offices or other state offices. A call to the appropriate UPO will provide you with necessary details.

Some county probate courts can be a source of unclaimed inheritances that can go into the millions of dollars. The inheritances are unclaimed because the court cannot find the heirs listed in the decedent's *will* or the *decedent* died without a will (*intestate*).

> **Will:** The legal statement of a person's wishes about what shall be done with his property after death. It usually must be in writing.
>
> **Decedent:** A person who has died.
>
> **Intestate:** The condition of having made no will.

State laws spell out who can inherit if the decedent dies intestate. Wives, children, aunts, uncles and first cousins can inherit in all states. In some states anyone who is a blood relative can inherit.

The average size of an estate today is around $75,000 to $150,000. On average, someone who dies between the ages of 65 and 80 will own a home, furniture, stamp or coin collection, car, have a bank account and own some type of securities, such as mutual funds, stocks or bonds.

When the full value of the estate is determined, it is almost always worth at least $100,000.

The only *federal agency* that will allow a finder's fee is the Federal Housing Authority (FHA). To obtain the fee, you must locate the people who had FHA home loans who now have mortgage insurance refunds due to them. Your fee will be a percentage of the refund and will be collected from the people you find. The amounts of these refunds are usually small and are not as profitable as unclaimed assets listed by the state UPOs and probate courts.

The Steps in Heir Searching

1. Find out about new accounts or new cases. This can be done by the searcher or by a *reporter.*

    Reporter: A person who locates cases in
    probate courts and usually receives 5% if
    the case is successful.

2. Locate heirs or rightful owners. Find an address and telephone number by computer searches, manual searches of new and old telephone books, city directories, court records, tax records, etc.
3. Contact individuals and verify that they are the legal heir or rightful owner.
4. Present agreement to heirs and secure their signature. This is done by certified mail, fax, Federal Express or in person.
5. Present agreement to unclaimed property division, or in probate cases hire an attorney to petition the court for the inheritance.

6. Assist the UPO, probate court, or attorney in securing any information required to prove claim (e.g. certified birth certificate, census records, marriage certificates, death certificates, annulments, drivers licenses, social security cards, etc.)

7. Determine status of claim periodically.

8. As soon as finder's fee is received, send appropriate share to professionals who helped you (e.g. reporter, attorney).

9. Secure authorization from heir of testimonial for use in future cases.

Time Line

A case starts when an amount of unclaimed money is identified. That case ends when your finder's fee and all the other fees are *disbursed*. The total time to complete a case varies greatly in different states and jurisdictions.

> **Disbursement:** When the final accounting is made and the different fees are paid.

As an example:

January. An heir searcher identifies a probate case.
February. Heir searcher identifies and locates the heirs.
March. Heirs sign the *contract*.
April. The attorney makes this information available to the court.

> **Contract/agreement:** A document between the potential rightful owner or heir and the heir searcher, outlining the finder's fee.

From here, it will take an average of six weeks to secure certified birth certificates, census reports, marriage, divorce and death documentation, and anything else required by the court to establish the relationship and right to the inheritance. Since most court dockets are full, it can take anywhere from two to eighteen months for the courts to examine the evidence and rule on the petition. Sometimes before disbursement is made, decisions must be made by tax authorities concerning *inheritance tax* and income tax payments. After these steps have been successfully completed, disbursements to heirs and the heir searchers are concurrently made (everybody is paid at one time). The total time process can be up to two years. However, a few cases in some jurisdictions may take as long as three years to complete.

Inheritance tax: A tax levied by the state
upon beneficiaries.

Full-Time or Part-Time Profession

Heir searching can be either a full-time profession or a part-time job. The only problem is that you may not get your first "paycheck" for two years. Therefore, it is important to realize that you must be able to support yourself by some other means for up to two years.

There are numerous heir searching organizations that have been in business for many years. They employ several individuals and also have business arrangements with other heir searchers, reporters, researchers and attorneys. Additionally, there are many one-person operations who do heir searching as a full-time or part-time activity. Many private investigators, *genealogists*, researchers and others moonlight as heir searchers. The common denominator for all of these heir searchers is that they all are making money from this enterprise.

> **Genealogist**: A person who studies the
> ancestry and lineage of families.

Personal Requirements of Heir Searching

1. **Time.** It can take a lot of time to properly find out about unclaimed money and to locate the legal owners. You must be patient and willing to work long hours, and you must have adequate time to perform these functions, if you are going to be successful. This is not a get-rich-quick business. But on the other hand, there have been several people who have made a great deal of money in a relatively short time. This is the exception rather than the rule.

2. **Effort.** This work can be tedious, difficult and time consuming. You must be thorough but also efficient. Most of the time it is not easy to locate the missing heirs or they would have been found by now.

3. **Money.** As usual, you have to spend money to make money. You will have to set yourself up to begin with: office equipment, stationery, brochures, etc. You may end up with a hefty long distance telephone bill. You will have to pay for postage, including special charges when you must have something there "overnight." Sometimes you will have to meet with someone in person, so you will need to allow for travel expenses.

You must pay other professionals for services you cannot perform yourself. Buying a "list of accounts" is another necessary expense.

4. **Computers and databases.** In today's modern age, searchers must have a computer with a modem and a CD-ROM reader. You must also subscribe to databases to obtain the most current information available (see Appendix C for information on databases.) A computer is also the best way to keep track of your cases and what information you have confirmed.

5. **Fax, phone and answering machine.** You must be able to communicate and do it quickly. Most of the time it is best to see information in writing, and the fastest way to do this is with a fax. Some computers can perform this function.

6. **Books on searching.** There are a few books available on the subject of heir searching, and many books you need as research tools. As a minimum, a searcher needs the following:

   • *National ZIP Code Directory*
   • *United States Atlas* (also available on CD-Rom)
   • *Find Anyone Fast by Phone, Fax, Mail and Computer*
   • *How to Locate Anyone Who Is or Has Been in the Military*
   • *How to Investigate by Computer.*

7. **Business license and private investigator license.** Some states will require you to have one or both of these to obtain information and to perform searches.

8. **Space.** You will need an office to properly keep track

of all the paper and computer information required for each case. If you cannot create an office in your home, you will have to rent an office, thus increasing your expense.

Duties

An heir searcher should be familiar with the following duties or jobs. If you are unable to perform these duties yourself, you may have to contact a professional who specializes in these areas.

Reporter. Locates cases in probate courts. If you act as a reporter for someone else, you will usually receive 5% if the case is successful.

Researcher. Searches vital records for correct spelling of names, DOB, SSN, old and current addresses and other pertinent information

Census researcher. Specifically studies census information (federal, state and city) to obtain names, ages, and location of relatives. If you do this for someone else, you can charge an hourly fee, or a percentage.

Locator. Determines current address and telephone number of heirs or eligible recipients, usually by computer. This can be accomplished by phone, letter and fax.

In most states an attorney cannot be an heir searcher. You will have to hire an attorney at some point to file claim in appropriate probate courts. He will represent both you and the heir. The attorney receives an hourly fee or a percentage. This is established before the attorney does any work. To locate a probate attorney, call the city or county bar association in the area where the claim must be filed. You can also contact probate courts for names of probate attorneys who have handled cases in their jurisdiction.

Attitude of Others

Many state government employees frown on heir searchers. They do not recognize that a legal and useful service is being provided. Often, this is because their own people are not doing a very good job at locating people who are entitled to abandoned money. Other states have a more favorable attitude about heir searchers. Keep in mind that the work heir searchers do, is legal, ethical and a service to many people.

Networking

You may be able to find the rightful owner to some unclaimed money without anyone else's help. However, you will, at one time or another, need the services of other professionals. Many times it is wise and prudent to enter into an agreement with another heir searcher who is expert in other subjects such as military, other states, census information, etc. Once you have reached an agreement, you are considered associates. Some helpers offer their services for free, e.g. librarians, agents in abandoned property offices, and probate court clerks. Some work on an hourly or per case basis, e.g. genealogists, professional researchers, computer experts, vital statistics researchers and census researchers.

Most attorneys will work by the hour, or they may request 8–10% of the total amount. If you enter into an agreement with another heir searcher the normal agreement is for a 50/50 split of the finder's fee (after all expenses have been paid).

Competition

There is a great deal of competition in this profession. Many individuals and firms have been doing heir searching for a long time. They are very good at finding and signing up heirs. The larger the amount of the unclaimed estate or property, the more competition there will be to find the rightful owner first. So, do not expect to be the only one who is searching a particular case. You must be properly prepared to do research, have the proper tools and be prepared to act rapidly if you are to be successful. You must be the first one to find and notify the rightful owner. If you do find the rightful owners and they say they have already been contacted by someone, see what percentage they have been offered and attempt to underbid. First prize goes to the heir searcher who obtains a signed agreement. There are no prizes for second place in this business.

Usually, the only way you will find out if someone else is working on the same case is by accident. If you call the VA about an individual and they say they have had two calls about this already, you know you are not the only one working the case.

Few searchers will be interested in estates or abandoned money accounts that are worth only $200 to $500. When you compare the amount of the finder's fee that can be obtained to the expense of locating the rightful owner, it may seem that it is not profitable to work small cases. However, if all the big dogs are going for the big cases, why not work the small ones. Keep in mind that you not only have little or no competition but you can get bigger finder's fees.

Ethics

Ethics is one of the most important things to keep in mind if you are going to be a successful heir searcher. This is one business where the phrase "my word is my bond" must hold true. In your dealings with other heir searchers, it is imperative that you be honest and keep your promises. Whether the agreement is verbal or written, if you promise a fellow heir searcher that you will split the finder's fee 50/50 with him, you had better give him that percentage when disbursement is made. To do otherwise could not only cause you legal hassles and result in the loss of business contacts, but it could also ruin your reputation throughout the industry in a very short time.

When dealing with heirs, you must also be honest. Let them know you are a professional and that this is a legitimate claim. Suggest they have a lawyer look over the contract. Offer business references they can call to check out your credentials.

Do not volunteer the sources you used to locate them. If they ask, be honest and explain that you cannot reveal the source of the funds because they can go around you directly to that source. However, you should not exaggerate any facts to entice them to sign an agreement. (North Carolina law requires that the finder disclose the whereabouts of the money in the contract.)

It is not necessary to volunteer the exact amount of money involved, especially since that amount may change due to fees or other heirs that may be found. It is perfectly ethical to say that you have located a small, modest or a large sum of money that may belong to them.

Brochure

A well done, professionally prepared brochure is essential to establishing good rapport with your customers. This will show that you are a professional, that the claim is legitimate, etc. You should include memberships in professional organizations, such as the Chamber of Commerce, Better Business Bureau, etc. A first impression is a lasting impression

Conclusion

This has been a brief explanation of heir searching. There is a great deal of detailed information that you must learn on your own. Some will be obtained as you do your first searches; other information can sometimes be obtained from experienced searchers. You should make arrangements with a local probate attorney to handle the cases you obtain in your county or state. You should ask him about state inheritance laws, inheritance taxes, wills, court procedures and requirements. You can visit the local bar association or law school library and read up on these subjects. You also should spend time in your local public library where there is a wealth of information that can help you.

This profession is a beautiful opportunity for many. There is good money to be made for those who can do the job right and who can do it quickly.

Chapter Seven

State requirements
for heir searchers

As shown on the following pages, each state has different requirements for heir searchers. Many states require you to have a private investigator's license to do this type of work. Some states will not sell you the list of accounts unless you are licensed by that particular state. In some states you must have a current business license. Check with the appropriate Unclaimed Property Offices to be sure you know what the current requirements are. These requirements can change at any time.

ALABAMA
The state of Alabama does not regulate heir searchers and the state does not allow the public to come to their office and view their records. Heir searchers who have a contract with a client must have power of attorney and affidavit of non-revocation.

Note: The only list available is the list of names published in the statewide newspapers. This is published
every spring and fall.

Maximum finder's fee: Not regulated

ALASKA

There are no restrictions for heir searching in Alaska.
Anyone can purchase a list of names. A list may be
bought on computer disk for $10 or photocopies start at
$30 on up. Please contact the state for exact price. The list
is published once a year. Last known address, dollar
amount of assets held, and the date the assets were acquired are recorded in the unclaimed property list.

Maximum finder's fee: Not regulated

ARIZONA

Arizona requires heir searchers to have an Arizona private investigator's license. A list is not available, however
they do allow heir searchers to view the files in their
Phoenix or Tucson offices. The state will not disclose information on accounts that are less than two years old.
Computer information contains name of individual, last
known address and the date the assets were acquired. The
dollar amount is not listed.

Maximum finder's fee: 30%

ARKANSAS

Any resident of the state of Arkansas can access the computer files in the state Unclaimed Property Office. The
computer information contains the name, last known
address and amount of money held by the state. A print-

ed list is only available from the newspaper listing.

Maximum finder's fee: 10%

CALIFORNIA

California requires heir searchers to be licensed private investigators in the state. A list is available for $300 with update costs of $75. Lists are published twice a year. The list contains names, last known address, and amount of money held.

Maximum finder's fee: 10%

COLORADO

Anyone may a purchase a list of unclaimed property owners in Colorado. The cost is $120 if you pick it up from their office or $125 if mailed. The list contains names, last known addresses, holder's name, amount of money held by the state and when the state acquired the property.

Maximum finder's fee: Not regulated

CONNECTICUT

Information for unclaimed property accounts is open to the public. No license is required. A list of names and last known addresses is available from the state. Prices vary; please contact their office for current price. Connecticut does not disclose accounts that are less than two years old.

Maximum finder's fee: 10%

DELAWARE

There are no regulations regarding heir searching other than having a business license. A private investigator's license is not required. There are no lists available. The listing published in October in statewide newspapers is the only information available. The list has the name of the individual, last known address, and name of the holder.

Maximum finder's fee: Not regulated

DISTRICT OF COLUMBIA

The District of Columbia requests all heir searchers to send for an information package, which explains all guidelines. A list cannot be purchased. The only list available is the names and last known addresses that are published twice a year in the newspapers. District of Columbia does not disclose accounts until a year after acquisition.

Maximum finder's fee: 10%

FLORIDA

To perform heir searching in Florida you must have a Florida private investigator's license. A list can be obtained in person by using one of seven computer terminals available in the Unclaimed Property Office, or information is available on microfiche ($30) or computer tape ($90-120). The list has name of owner, last known address, SSN (if available), amount of money and holder's name.

Maximum finder's fee: Not regulated

GEORGIA

Anyone may purchase a list from the Unclaimed Property Office. To receive the information on computer disk the cost is $50 and fills approximately 7 disks. The report contains tracking numbers, names of individuals, and holder's name. Georgia holds all accounts for two years from date of acquisition. A private investigator's license is not required, but it is recommended to check with the Secretary of State's office before pursuing heir searching.

Maximum finder's fee: 10%

HAWAII

There are no requirements for heir searching in Hawaii. Anyone may purchase a list for $450. The information is updated daily and has name of individual, last known address, and amount of money acquired.

Maximum finder's fee: 20%

IDAHO

Idaho does not publish a list other than the newspaper notice. Anyone is allowed to view records in the Unclaimed Property Office. Names and last known addresses are included in the files. They hold all new accounts for two years.

Maximum finder's fee: Not regulated

ILLINOIS

A private investigator's license is required for heir searching in Illinois. However, they do not sell a list of names.

The state library has a microfiche list of names and addresses only. This list is updated annually. New names are published in newspapers in February and August.

Maximum finder's fee: 10%

INDIANA

Indiana has no licensing requirements for searchers. A copy of the contract with the owner is requested so that they can enforce the maximum finder's fee regulation.

Maximum finder's fee: 10%

IOWA

An Iowa private investigator's license is required to perform heir searching. No list is available for purchase. However, microfiche is available for research in the Unclaimed Property Office. When contracts are written, they must disclose amount, location and nature of property. The state holds all accounts for two years.

Maximum finder's fee: 15%

KANSAS

No regulation for searchers in Kansas. The only information that can be obtained is from the newspaper listing, which has names and last known addresses. Kansas prohibits searchers from access to information for the first two years the state has the money.

Maximum finder's fee: 15%

KENTUCKY

Kentucky does not regulate heir searching. Anyone may purchase an unclaimed property list for $26.33 per year. No information is available from before 1991.

Maximum finder's fee: Not regulated

LOUISIANA

Heir searchers must have a Louisiana private investigator's license. No list is available for purchase, however, you may search the records in their office. The unclaimed property records contain the names, last known addresses and the date the assets were acquired by the state. The amount of money is not available.

Maximum finder's fee: 10%

MAINE

Maine does not regulate heir searchers. The list is available for the public to view in the Unclaimed Property Office. The list has name of individual, last known address and amount of money held.

Maximum finder's fee: 15%

MARYLAND

Heir searching is not regulated in this state. A list is available for a base fee of $500 with additional costs depending on the amount of data requested. The list contains name of individual, last known address, and the date the assets were acquired by the state. A contract is not enforceable if the money found is less than two years old.

Maximum finder's fee: Not regulated

MASSACHUSETTS

Depending on the circumstances, a private investigator's license may be required. Please check the Office of Unclaimed Property for further information. Massachusetts does not disclose accounts until after a two- year waiting period. A list is available on microfiche for years 1981-1992. The charge is $10 per year. Name, last known address, dollar amount and the date the assets were acquired is included on the report.

Maximum finder's fee: 10%

MICHIGAN

A private investigator's license is required for searchers in Michigan. A list is available from the office of unclaimed property and the cost is determined by the type of information requested. Please contact them directly for further information. The list includes name, last known address, dollar amount of assets, and the date the assets were acquired. It does not include Social Security numbers.

Maximum finder's fee: 5%

MINNESOTA

There is no regulation of heir searching in Minnesota. Anyone may go to the Unclaimed Property Office and view records. No list is available for purchase; the listing printed in statewide newspapers is the only printed list.

Maximum finder's fee: 10%

MISSISSIPPI

Heir searchers are not required to be licensed or registered to do business in Mississippi. A list is available for $250 plus postage and handling.

Maximum finder's fee: Not regulated

MISSOURI

Missouri does not require a private investigator's license, but they do require heir searchers to have the appropriate business licenses and to register with their office. A list is available for $1500. The list has names and last known addresses.

Maximum finder's fee: 35%

MONTANA

Montana has no state regulations for heir searchers. The only list obtainable by the general public is the list published in the statewide newspapers.

Maximum finder's fee: Not regulated

NEBRASKA

There are no licensing requirements for Nebraska. The state does not release information on accounts until after a 24 month waiting period. The records can be viewed by appointment only.

Maximum finder's fee: 10%

NEVADA

Nevada requires searchers to have a Nevada private investigator's license. Please contact the state Unclaimed

Property Office for the current price of the list. The records can be viewed in person by appointment. These records contain name, last known address, dollar amounts and the date the assets were acquired.

Maximum finder's fee: 10%

NEW HAMPSHIRE

Anyone may purchase a list of unclaimed property accounts. New Hampshire does not regulate professional searchers. Please contact the Unclaimed Property Office directly for a current price list. The list has name, last known address and the date the assets were acquired by the state. It does not list dollar amounts.

Maximum finder's fee: Not regulated

NEW JERSEY

New Jersey has no regulations for finders and no list is available. The only source of information is the listing in county newspapers which gives names and last known addresses. A 24 month holding period is enforced for all new accounts.

Maximum finder's fee: 20%

NEW MEXICO

A private investigator's license is not needed, but you must be registered with the state. The list is available for sale. Please check with the office for a current price.

Maximum finder's fee: No set fee. The average is 35%.

NEW YORK

New York state does not require any licensing to perform heir searching. A complete list is obtainable under the Freedom of Information Act. Contact their office directly for prices. The list contains name, last known address and the date the assets were acquired by the state.

Maximum finder's fee: Not regulated

NORTH CAROLINA

A North Carolina private investigator's license is required to perform heir searching in this state. However, contracts with owners must state the nature of the money, the value of the property, the holder's name, and where the funds are held. Due to this fact there are not many professional finders working in North Carolina. A list can be purchased directly from the Unclaimed Property Office. Please call for a current price list.

Maximum finder's fee: 25%

NORTH DAKOTA

Anyone may purchase a list of unclaimed property owners. A contract between owners and finders is not enforceable if the finder is not a licensed private investigator. Contact their office for cost of the list and availability. The list contains names, last known addresses, amount of money held, and the date the assets were acquired by the state.

Maximum finder's fee: 25%

OHIO
Ohio does not regulate heir searchers. Anyone may purchase the list. Please call their office for price and availability of the list. The list is published once a year.
Maximum finder's fee: 10%

OKLAHOMA
There are no license requirements for heir searchers in Oklahoma. Anyone may purchase or view the records of unclaimed property. The list is updated twice a year. Power of attorney and a finder's fee contract is required when submitting claim information.
Maximum finder's fee: 25%

OREGON
Oregon has no license requirements for heir searching. The list is available to the general public and be purchased; please contact their office for complete details. No account is disclosed to searchers until the 24 month waiting period has elapsed. The list contains name, address, and the amount of money held by the state. A subscription list is available giving names already contacted.
Maximum finder's fee: None

PENNSYLVANIA
Pennsylvania does not require a searcher to have a private investigator's license. The list is available for searchers. Contact their office in writing for cost and availability. The list contains names and last known addresses. There is a 24 month waiting period on new accounts.
Maximum finder's fee: 10%

RHODE ISLAND

There are no laws in Rhode Island regulating heir searchers. The list is not for sale. The newspaper listing is the only source of names available to searchers.

Maximum finder's fee: None

SOUTH CAROLINA

South Carolina requires a private investigator's license for heir searchers. A list can be obtained on microfiche. Contact their office for current price. All new accounts are held for a 24 month waiting period before information is disclosed to searchers.

Maximum finder's fee: 15%

SOUTH DAKOTA

Heir searching is not regulated in South Dakota. The list is not for sale. Check the newspapers for the list of names.

Maximum finder's fee: 25%

TENNESSEE

Tennessee's unclaimed property list is open to anyone. There are no license requirements pertaining to heir searching. A microfiche list can be purchased for $30 or you may view records for free in the office. The list contains, names last known address, and the amount of money held.

Maximum finder's fee: 10%

TEXAS

All heir searchers must have a Texas private investigator's license. A list is available on microfiche. Check with the Unclaimed Property Office for the current price. The list has names, last known addresses, and the amount of unclaimed money.

Maximum finder's fee: 10%

UTAH
Utah does not regulate finders. A list is available, but check with their office for the current price. The name, last known address, and amount of unclaimed money is included in the list.

Maximum finder's fee: Not regulated

VERMONT
Anyone may perform heir searching in Vermont. A private investigator's license is not required. A list may be obtained from the state office for $90 plus postage. The list has names, last known addresses, amount of money, and the date when the state acquired the money.

Maximum finder's fee: Not regulated

VIRGINIA
Virginia does not have any regulations concerning heir finders. No lists are available other than the names published in the newspapers.

Maximum finder's fee: Not regulated

WASHINGTON
A business license is needed for heir searchers. There are no lists for sale, but records can be viewed in the Unclaimed Property Office. The Washington Information System has terminals in malls that are available to the

general public. The information available is name, last known address, holder's name, and a range of the amount of money held. Contact their office for an heir searcher's information package.

Maximum finder's fee: 5%

WEST VIRGINIA
West Virginia does not provide a list. There are no regulations for searchers in this state. The newspaper listing has names, last known addresses, account number and holder's name.

Maximum finder's fee: Not regulated

WISCONSIN
Anyone may purchase a list of unclaimed property owners in Wisconsin. There are no license requirements. Contact their office for prices. The list has name, last known address, dollar amount of assets, and the date the assets were acquired by the state.

Maximum finder's fee: 20%

WYOMING
Wyoming does not have any regulations or license requirements for heir searching. A list can be purchased with names, last known addresses, amount of money, and the date the assets were acquired by the state. Contact their office for the current price.

Maximum finder's fee: Searcher and owner can set price.

Chapter Eight

Contracts and agreements

A contract or agreement is the signed document between the potential rightful owner or heir and the heir searcher. It states that the owner relinquishes to the heir searcher a percentage of the money he is due. This is the finder's fee and it is due to the heir searcher because he has located the assets and the rightful owner. The document usually specifies that all fees related to acquiring the inheritance/account will be absorbed by the heir searcher and not paid by the owner.

An agreement normally states that the searcher may obtain the services of an attorney, also at no cost to the heir. These agreements are considered as legal contracts and once signed, the heir cannot "go around" the heir searcher and claim the money. Such an event would constitute a breach of contract and the heir could be forced to pay the finder's fee and other costs.

The following is a sample cover letter and agreement.

(Letterhead)

(Date)

Mr. John Doe
123 Home Street
Miami, FL 39348

Dear Mr. Doe:

We have located a small sum of money that may
be due to you.

Our company locates missing people who are
due money that they do not know about. We receive a percentage of all money received.

Our company is listed with Dun and Bradstreet
and we are a member of the Milwaukee Retail
Merchants Association. For the latter, you
may contact Phyllis Smith at (414) 555-4938,
1801 Broadway, Milwaukee, WI 58111.

I have enclosed two copies of our agreement
concerning obtaining the money due to you.
Please call me collect if you have any questions. Otherwise, please sign one copy of the
agreement and mail it to me immediately in the
enclosed envelope. Keep the other copy for
your records.

After I receive your signed agreement, I will
notify you of the source of this money and the
amount you will receive. It is very important
that you sign and return the agreement as soon
as possible to ensure that you receive your
share in a timely manner.

I look forward to receiving your signed
agreement.

Sincerely,

Michael J. Bryant
President

To: Acme Investigative Research
      PO Box 94628
      Milwaukee, WI 58167

In consideration of your having brought to my attention the undersigned certain assets to which I may have an interest, the nature of which is to be disclosed to me by Acme Investigative Research;

And in consideration of the work to date and of further investigations to gather all information regarding my said claim, I do hereby assign to Acme Investigative Research an amount equal to ____ percent (__%) of whatever net proceeds I receive, now and in the future, as a result of your efforts solely with regard to this one claim only, subject to the following conditions:

1. Acme Investigative Research is obligated to pay all expenses to prove my claim and I will not have to advance any moneys toward their effort.
2. Acme Investigative Research is authorized to retain an attorney at no cost to me to represent my interest and to collect all assets due to me and said attorney's fees shall not be deducted from my assets hereunder.
3. If I receive no assets, Acme Investigative Re search will likewise receive nothing and this agreement shall be deemed null and void.
4. Acme Investigative Research is further autho rized to act as my agent in order to process and collect any funds due to me regarding this matter.

Dated this ____ day of _____, 19__.

_____
Signature and Name (Please print)

_____
Address

_____
City, State, Zip

Additional Forms

After you have obtained a signed agreement from an heir, you may need to send one or more of the following forms. These forms should be used in all probate cases and in some unclaimed property cases.

Acknowledgement of Disclosure

After you receive the signed agreement from the heir and notify them of the source of the money, have them sign an Acknowledgement of Disclosure (page 138). This form is prepared by the heir searcher. The attorney selected to represent the heir presents this document to the court to prove that the heir was told the source of the money.

Attorney Representation Agreement

If an attorney is necessary, such as for a probate case, the heir searcher selects the attorney to represent the heir. Even though the attorney is paid by the heir searcher, out of the finder's fee, he does not represent the heir searcher. An Attorney Representation Agreement is usually prepared by the attorney, but may also be prepared the the heir searcher (page 139). The purpose of this agreement is for the heir to acknowledge that the named attorney will represent him in the heir case. This document may not be required in all cases, but it is recommended that the heir searcher use it whenever possible. Some heirs have been able to go around the heir searcher because this agreement was not signed. If the heir is successful in obtaining the inheritance without paying the finder's fee, the heir searcher can sue the heir for breach of contract.

Family History Form

The Family History Form is a very important document (page 140). It is used by the heir searcher and the probate court to assist in verifying that the individual who signed the contract is related to the decedent and qualifies to inherit the estate. This should not be presented to the heir until the Agreement, the Acknowledgement of Disclosure and the Attorney Representation Agreement have been received.

Many state Unclaimed Property Offices require a specific contract or agreement. The appropriate state Unclaimed Property Office should be contacted to acquire a sample document. New heir searchers should discuss the matter of agreements with an attorney who specializes in probate matters. The best attorney would be one who has worked with other heir searchers.

It is extremely important that a legal and proper agreement be used. Many heir searchers have lost their finder's fees by not using agreements that were in accordance with the appropriate laws.

ACKNOWLEDGEMENT OF DISCLOSURE

I hereby acknowledge that, subsequent to exe-
cuting my Agreement with _____
which is dated this _____ day of _____, 19__,
they informed me that the estate from which I
may receive a possible inheritance is that of
(name of estate), late of (court).

With full information concerning the source of
the possible inheritance, I now ratify and
confirm the above agreement.

Dated this _____ day of _____, 19_____.

_____
Witness

                _____
                Heir Name

                _____
                Address

                _____
                City, State, Zip

ATTORNEY REPRESENTATION AGREEMENT

(Attorney)
(Firm)
(Address)
(City, State, Zip)

RE: The Estate of _____

Dear Mr. _____:

I agree to have you represent me and enter an
appearance on my behalf in the above captioned
estate. In this capacity you will endeavor to
prove my relationship as an heir at law to the
estate and to process and collect any funds
due me. It is my understanding that you will be
paid directly by _____. I will have no
obligation to pay you directly.

Dated this ____ day of _____, 19__.

_____
Witness   Heir Name

                                 _____
                                 Address

                                 _____
                                 City, State, Zip

Family History Form

Re: The Estate of: _____

1. Your full name:_____

2. Place of birth:_____

3. Date of birth:_____

4. Place of all marriages:_____

5. Date of all marriages:_____

6. Name of spouse's (including maiden name):_____

   _____

7. Name of father:_____

8. Name of mother:_____

9. Parent's place of marriage:_____

10. Father's place of death:_____

11. Mother's place of death:_____

12. Name of grandfather:_____

13. His place of death:_____

14. Name of grandmother:_____

15. Her place of death:_____

16. Names of brothers and sisters:

    _____

    _____

    _____

17. If deceased, please list any children they had:
    (include address)

    _____

18. Your Social Security number:_____

19. Your telephone number: (____)_____

Chapter Nine

Case studies

This chapter contains examples of cases solved by heir searchers. The first two were solved by the author.

I do a lot of work for one of the oldest heir searching firms in the country. They have an agreement with several mutual fund institutions. In January of 1991, they contacted me about a case worth over $115,000 in mutual funds. The only information available was the individual's name and his military address in Vietnam during the war. I made numerous calls to the Department of Veterans Affairs but was unable to find any mention of him in their files. I also contacted the National Personnel Records Center. The name was too common to pursue that angle. Since I had been unable to find a military connection, I thought he might have been a civil service employee. I contacted a librarian who does research for me and she was able to find a CORDS Register. CORDS was an agency in Vietnam made up mostly of civil service employees from the State Department and the Department of Agriculture. She found his name and where he went to college. I contacted the college and determined his date of birth. I then checked the Social Security Death Index (SSDI) and found out when and where he had died. I obtained a copy of his obituary from the library in the city listed on the SSDI. The obituary stated that he was a widower and had four children, one of whom was living in the town where he died. I used the National Telephone Directory to get her address and phone number. I contacted her and verified that he had been assigned to CORDS and had spent ten years in Vietnam. I passed all of this information on to the heir searching firm who then contacted all of the children. Each of them refused to sign the contract. They thought they could find the money themselves. After two years, they realized they could not locate the money and signed the contract. Several months later, I received a check for $12,000.

One of the most interesting cases I have solved started when I was contacted by a professional heir searcher in New York state. He said he had an unusual case. A man had died in Virginia and left an estate worth slightly over one million dollars. He was divorced, had no children, and was born in Washington, DC. A check of the newspapers in Washington produced two stories in 1943 about the decedent's father. One described how he had stolen an ocelot from the Washington Zoo. He went to a local bar to show the animal to a friend. While there, the ocelot scratched the man. He attempted to strangle it, but when that failed to kill it, he drowned it in the sink at the bar. The bartender called the police, who arrested the man. The other story referred to this incident and that the man had had an argument with his wife. Extensive research had been directed by the probate court to locate this father or any heirs. A well qualified searcher had done painstaking and extensive research, but without success. Letters and calls were made to numerous federal and state agencies including the Social Security Administration, but all were negative. When I received the researcher's report and studied the case, I had a hunch that the father had probably gone to California. I contacted an associate in California who checked the state death files and found the he had died in Los Angeles in 1982. When a copy of his obituary was obtained from the Los Angeles Times, it stated that the father was survived by a son who lived in the Los Angeles area. My associate obtained the son's address from the funeral home and sent it to me by fax. When I called the son, I found that the father had married again after he moved to California. The son was the half-brother of the decedent. His father had never spoken about the son in Virginia. He immediately signed an agreement as he had no idea where the money was from. He received over $660,000. The New York heir searcher and I split the finder's fee in half, each receiving $150,000. I then had to write my associate in California a check for $75,000. All in all, I did not have to do that much work for my $75,000.

Here are some cases solved by other heir searchers.

Michael Baker recently died in a veterans hospital in a southern city. He was buried in the local National Cemetery because he was a veteran. The only ones who attended his funeral were the representatives from the funeral home and the patient representative of the VA hospital. He apparently had no relatives. It was determined that his estate was worth over $150,000. Most of this money was from disability payments he received from the VA. His records at the VA showed he had never married. There were no records of any relatives. John Hurst is a part-time heir searcher and he was alerted to the case by the VA representative. John sent a Standard Form 180 to the National Personnel Records Center requesting copies of Michael's military records. He was told that Michael's records had been destroyed in a fire in 1973. He also asked for Michael's records from the VA. When these arrived, they contained only his death certificate and several letters concerning his claim for disabilities. There was no information about any relatives in these VA records. Michael's death certificate did not list his parents' names. John decided to send off for Michael's original application for a Social Security card (SS-2) from the Social Security Administration. Several weeks later it arrived. This document listed both his mother's and father's names and where he had applied for a Social Security card. John checked the 1920 census and located entries on his parents. The census also showed that he had a brother named Ralph who was five years old. Since the census was taken in 1920, the brother would have been born around 1915. Michael was able to determine from the Social Security Master Death Index that Ralph died in 1985 in Sun City, AZ. He checked the newspapers in Phoenix and Sun City for Ralph's obituary. It stated that he was survived by a son, Ralph Baker,

Jr. of Sweetwater, Texas. John found the son by calling the information operator in Sweetwater and obtaining his telephone number and address. He sent the son an agreement for 35%. The son signed and returned the agreement immediately. Both were very happy with the arrangement and they each received their shares within the year.

Denise Brolin lived in Austin, Texas where she had a job in a government office. Once a week, she would visit the state Unclaimed Property Office and find out if there were any new cases whose value was over $20,000. She "reported" these cases to a large heir searching firm. Over the last three years, Denise has made over $40,000 a year as a reporter.

Robby Lindsey was a traveling salesman for a large pharmaceutical supply company and a part-time probate reporter. His territory included twenty counties in the state in which he lived. He would call on drug stores in these counties; many were near the county courthouse. After he called on these drug stores he would visit the courthouse and check for new estates. Robby also became friendly with the clerks in the probate courts. They agreed to call him when new estates came in which the heirs could not be located. He was able to report over fifteen estates. The total value of these estates was over $2 million. The heir searcher he worked with was able to locate and receive agreements from the missing heirs for half of these cases. Robby received nearly $50,000 for his work as a reporter.

Sid Jaworsky was a veteran who died in 1992 in Florida. He left an estate worth over $400,000. His death certificate stated that he had never married. It did not contain either of his parents' names but did say he was born in Poland. Heir searcher, Scott McDonald was contacted by one of the nation's largest professional heir searching firms to handle this case for their company. Scott requested copies of Sid's military personnel records from the National Personnel Records Center under the Freedom of Information Act. He also requested copies of Sid's VA records. The military records failed to reveal the names of any relatives. However, the VA files did contain a letter from the veteran's mother in Poland that was sent to his doctor while he was in the hospital. With this information, an heir searching firm in Europe was notified. They located several cousins in Poland. All of them signed agreements and after two years, the heirs and the heir searchers shared in the disbursement of this $400,000 estate.

A large estate was located by an heir searching firm on the east coast. The estate consisted of government bonds worth almost $375,000. The only know heir was the son, but no one could locate him. Every available database was checked as were city directories, old telephone books and death records. Gabriel O'Connor was given the case by the east coast firm. He determined from the date of birth that the son may have served in the military during the Vietnam War. A check with the VA revealed that he had served in Vietnam and that he had changed his name. The VA computer database listed both names. Using the correct name, Gabriel quickly located the heir. He signed an agreement and, after one and a half years, received his inheritance less the finder's fee. The heir searching firm and Gabriel received 33.3% of the entire estate.

Lucy Sorbo, an heir searcher in Michigan, was contacted by James Pano, a private investigator/heir searcher from Florida. James had located an estate in Florida that was worth $90,000. He learned of it from the attorney for the estate. The decedent's nephew was to receive the entire estate if he could be located. Mr. Pano did not want any communication to come from Florida as he feared that the heir would easily figure out where the money was from. Lucy agreed to work on the case. She located the heir in the National Telephone Directory. She called the individual and told him he had some money due. She confirmed the heir's address and sent a letter and an agreement to him by Federal Express. The heir immediately signed the agreement and returned it to Lucy.

Renee Simons was an heir searcher who worked larger cases from the California abandoned property list. She began to search for the owner of an account worth $73,000. After several days, she found the owner on a computer database. She called and told him that she had found some money that was due to him. The owner replied that he had already been contacted by another heir searcher. Renee asked if he had signed an agreement. He said not yet. Renee asked what percentage the finder's fee was. The owner said it was for 40 percent. Renee said if he would sign an agreement with her, she would ask for only 35 percent. The man agreed and signed Renee's agreement.

Libby Riley was a clerk in a store that was directly across the street from the county courthouse. She learned about the opportunity of being a reporter from a professional heir searcher. Every working day during her lunch break, she went to the probate court. On each visit, she asked if any new cases had been received. In a year's time, she found four estates in which the administrators did not know the location of the heirs. She "reported" these cases to the heir searcher. He in turn was able to locate the heirs to three of the estates. His finder's fees amounted to over $100,000. Jane received $5,000 for finding these cases when the funds of the estates were distributed.

Tami Veltri was a professional genealogist. She liked this work but made very little money at it. She decided to become a part-time heir searcher. She received cases from an heir searcher she had done genealogy work for. They had a 50/50 split agreement. As she became more successful in this career, she purchased a computer and subscribed to an on-line locator service. This enabled her to solve a larger percentage of cases. After five years Tami is now making about $75,000 a year from heir searching.

Kaitlin Krause worked as a reporter for several years. She decided to try to solve some of the cases herself. She was successful with only two the first year. One of the estates was worth $15,000 and the other was worth $175,000. She netted over $30,000 for her efforts for her first year of work.

Jeff Cross has been an heir searcher for several years. He is an expert in locating American Indians. Another heir searcher called him one day. He had an estate worth over $200,000, but was unable to locate the heirs who were American Indians. They agreed on a 50/50 split if Jeff could locate the heirs. After two weeks, he located a first cousin and sent him an agreement. The heir signed the agreement that was for 30%. The attorney they hired received $16,000 while Jeff and the other heir searcher split $44,000.

Melinda Hughes was a secretary who worked part-time. She became interested in heir searching several years ago, and considered the idea of making a career out of this opportunity. She began as a reporter for an heir searcher and she made over $2,500 a year doing this. Later she decided to do her own research. For her first three cases as a full time heir searcher, she made over $125,000.

Ty Suhor was a professional heir searcher. He had a working arrangement with a probate attorney. The attorney handled all the cases for him that originated in their home state. One day the attorney told Ty about a new case. A wealthy man had died. He was single and did not have any apparent heirs. The case had not been sent to the probate court because there were some legal matters to take care of. Before the case was filed, Ty located a second cousin who was the only living heir. Ty secured an agreement for 40 percent. When the case was settled, Ty received over $46,000 because of a tip from his attorney.

Tom Sanders was a private investigator in a small town of 50,000 people. He had enough work to keep him busy for four to five hours a day. After talking to an heir searcher he had worked with, he decided to become a reporter. By visiting the local courthouse house and by talking to local probate attorneys, he learned of several cases. He passed this information on to the heir searcher. In three years he made an extra $65,000.

Lou Miller was a professional heir searcher in Florida. He visited several probate courts in Miami weekly. He learned of numerous cases. These cases varied in size from $10,000 to $500,000. Many could not be solved. Others were difficult and time consuming but could be solved. He often learned of cases where the heir's address was listed on the court papers, but the heir had not been contacted by the court or the administrators. These cases were quickly solved and brought in thousands of dollars a month.

Gilbert Baldwin is a private investigator who purchases the unclaimed property list from a southwestern state annually. The list contains several thousand names and the amount of money due to them. He specialized on the cases that are in the 10 to 20 thousand dollar range. The state allows him to collect a 10% finder's fee. On a good year, Gilbert's income is over $150,000.

Conclusion

Any questions or problems concerning possible claims should be directed to the appropriate state or federal agency. Since you must abide by their relevant laws and regulations, it is advisable to seek clarification or information from their offices directly or from an attorney.

You are strongly encouraged to obtain copies of *Find Anyone Fast by Phone, Fax, Mail and Computer* and *How to Locate Anyone Who Is or Has Been in the Military: Armed Forces Locator Guide*. These two books contain the principles used by successful heir searchers in locating missing heirs. Order information is included in the following pages.

I also encourage you to obtain the two computer access packages described in Appendix C. These are essential tools in locating the rightful owners and heirs of unclaimed money. In today's competitive world, you must have the proper tools that give you timely answers.

I would like to hear of your success stories and how you found unclaimed money belonging to you or others.

If you have any comments or suggestions that may affect future editions of this book, please write to us:

MIE PUBLISHING
PO Box 340081
San Antonio, TX 78234

Do not forget to check with the Unclaimed Property Offices again in a few years. The abandonment period varies from state to state. New accounts are always being added.

Appendix A

Directory of Unclaimed Property Offices

The following are the addresses of all 51 Unclaimed Property Offices. For your convenience, they have been set up for you to photocopy, make labels and attach to envelopes.

Alabama Dept. of Revenue
Unclaimed Property Section
PO Box 327580
Montgomery, AL 36132-7580

Alaska Department of Revenue
Unclaimed Property Section
PO Box 110420
Juneau, AK 99811-0420

Arizona Dept. of Revenue
Unclaimed Property
1600 West Monroe
Phoenix, AZ 85007-2650

Auditor of State
Unclaimed Property Division
103 West Capitol, Suite 805
Little Rock, AR 72201

Comptroller of the State of CA
Division of Collections
Bureau of Unclaimed Property
PO Box 942850
Sacramento, CA 94250-5873

Colorado State Treasury
Unclaimed Property Division
1560 Broadway, Suite 1225
Denver, CO 80202

Unclaimed Property Division
Connecticut State Treasury
PO Box 5665
Hartford, CT 06102

Delaware State Escheator
PO Box 8931
Wilmington, DE 19899

Office of the Comptroller
Unclaimed Property Unit
415 12th Street, NW #408
Washington, DC 20004

State Comptroller
Abandoned Property Section
State Capitol
Tallahassee, FL 32399-0350

Department of Revenue
Property Tax Division
Unclaimed Property Section
270 Washington St SW, Rm 404
Atlanta, GA 30334

Unclaimed Property Branch
Dept. of Budget & Finance
PO Box 150
Honolulu, HI 96810

Unclaimed Property
State Tax Commission
PO Box 36
Boise, ID 83722

Dept. of Financial Institutions
Unclaimed Property Division
500 Iles Park Place, Ste 510
Springfield, IL 62718

Office of Attorney General
Unclaimed Property Division
219 State House
Indianapolis, IN 46204-2794

Treasurer of State
Great Iowa Treasure Hunt
Hoover Building
Des Moines, IA 50319

State Treasurer
Unclaimed Property Division
900 SW Jackson, Suite 201
Topeka, KS 66612-1235

Kentucky Treasury Dept.
Capitol Annex, Suite 183
ATTN: Unclaimed Property
Frankfort, KY 40601

Unclaimed Property Section
Department of Revenue
PO Box 91010
Baton Rouge, LA 70821

Abandoned Property Division
Treasury Department
State Office Building
39 State House Street
Augusta, ME 04333-0039

Comptroller of the Treasury
Unclaimed Property Section
301 W. Preston Street
Baltimore, MD 21201

Treasury Department
Abandoned Property Division
1 Ash Burton Place, 12th Floor
Boston, MA 02108-1608

Department of Treasury
Escheats Division
Abandoned & Unclaimed
 Property Division
Lansing, MI 48922

Department of Commerce
Unclaimed Property
133 East 7th Street
St. Paul, MN 55101

Unclaimed Property Division
Mississippi Treasury Dept.
PO Box 138
Jackson, MS 39201

Unclaimed Property Division
PO Box 1004
Jefferson City, MO 65102-1272

State of Montana
Department of Revenue
Abandoned Property Section
PO Box 5805
Helena, MT 59620

Office of the State Treasurer
Unclaimed Property Division
State Capitol, Suite 2003
PO Box 94788
Lincoln, NE 68509

Dept. of Business & Industry
Unclaimed Property Division
2601 East Sahara Ave #270
Las Vegas, NV 89104

State Treasury
Div. of Abandoned Property
State House Annex, Room 205
Concord, NH 03301

Unclaimed Property
CN 214
Trenton, NJ 08646

Taxation & Revenue Dept.
Unclaimed Property Unit
PO Box 25123
Santa Fe, NM 87504-5123

Office/ State Comptroller
Office of Unclaimed Funds
9th Floor, A.E. Smith Bldg.
Albany, NY 12236

North Carolina, State Treasury
Escheat & Uncl. Prop. Program
325 N. Salisbury Street
Raleigh, NC 27603-1385

Unclaimed Property Division
PO Box 5523
Bismarck, ND 58502-5523

Division of Unclaimed Funds
77 South High Street, 20th Flr
Columbus, OH 43266-0545

Oklahoma Tax Commission
Unclaimed Property
2501 Lincoln Blvd
Oklahoma City, OK 73194-0010

Division of State Lands
Unclaimed Property Section
775 Summer Street, NE
Salem, OR 97310

State Treasurer
Office of Unclaimed Property
PO Box 1837
Harrisburg, PA 17105-1837

Unclaimed Property Division
PO Box 1435
Providence, RI 02901-1435

S. Carolina Dept of Revenue
Abandoned Property Div.
PO Box 125
Columbia, SC 29214

Unclaimed Property Division
State Treasury
500 East Capitol Avenue
Pierre, SD 57501-5070

State of Tennessee
Treasury Department
Unclaimed Property Division
9th Floor, Jackson Office Bldg
Nashville, TN 37243-0242

Texas Treasury
Unclaimed Property Division
PO Box 12019
Austin, TX 78711-2019

Unclaimed Property Division
Treasurer, State of Utah
341 South Main, 5th Floor
Salt Lake City, UT 84111

State Treasurer
Abandoned Property Division
Div. of Unclaimed Property
133 State Street, 2nd Floor
Montpelier, VT 05633-6200

Commonwealth of Virginia
Div. of Unclaimed Property
PO Box 2478
Richmond, VA 23207-2478

Department of Revenue
Special Programs Division
Unclaimed Property Section
PO Box 448
Olympia, WA 98507

State Treasurer's Office
Div. of Unclaimed Property
Bldg 1, Room E145
1900 Kanawha Blvd East
Charleston, WV 25305

State Treasurer's Office
Unclaimed Property Division
PO Box 2114
Madison, WI 53701-2114

122 West 25th Street
1st Floor West
 Herschler Building
Cheyenne, WY 82002

Appendix B

Locator services

The Nationwide Locator is a professional locator service that performs computer searches to provide addresses and other important information to the public. They provide information to heir searchers, attorneys, private investigators, collection agencies, reunion planners and others seeking information about friends or relatives. Their data is obtained from highly accurate and reasonably priced databases that contain information on over 160 million individuals.

An heir searcher may want to contact the Nationwide Locator to do one or two searches when they first start out. However, full-time searchers should obtain one or both computer access packages for their own searching instead of paying someone else. See Appendix C for information on these computer access packages.

Here are they types of searches the Nationwide Locator provides:

Social Security search

Provide a name and nine digit Social Security number (SSN) and receive the person's most current reported address, date reported and all previous reported addresses (if the SSN is contained in a national credit file). If a report of death has been submitted, it will be listed. $30 per SSN for a nationwide search.

Address update

Provide a name and last known address (not over ten years old) and receive the most current reported address and the names and telephone numbers of five neighbors. $30 per name submitted.

National Surname search

Provide a first name, middle initial and last name and the National Telephone Directory will be used to provide the names, addresses and listed telephone numbers of everyone in the nation with a matching name. $30 per name submitted.

Date of Birth search

Provide first and last name, approximate date or year of birth and Social Security number (if known) and receive all matching names, city and state of residence. May be able to provide street address and phone number. $75 per name and date of birth submitted.

Social Security Death Index search

Provide either the name and date of birth, name and Social Security number, or name only and receive a list of people who are deceased, their SSN, date of birth, and the date and place of death as reported by the Social Security Administration. $30 per name.

Information will be provided to you within 24 hours of receipt. Information will be returned by mail or by fax, if requested. Volume discounts are available. Prices are subject to change without notice. Other specialized searches are available. Texas residents add 7.75% tax.

> Client agrees that all information obtained through the Nationwide Locator will be used for lawful purposes and agrees to hold the Nationwide Locator harmless for any use of this service. Client states that the client understands and agrees the Nationwide Locator does not warrant and does not guarantee information obtained from database searches. Client agrees to pay for all searches made by the Nationwide Locator regardless of results (to include "no record"). The Nationwide Locator is owned by Military Information Enterprises, Inc., is a member of the San Antonio Retail Merchants Association and is listed by Dun and Bradstreet.

If you would like the Nationwide Locator to perform any of these searches, please write or fax the information required to perform the search along with the following:

1. Payment in full: check, money order or credit card. If using Visa, MasterCard or American Express, please include your card number, the expiration date, the amount charged, and your signature.

2. Your name

3. Your phone number

4. Your address, including city, state and zip code.

5. A self-addressed stamped business size envelope.

7. Fax number, if information is returned by fax.

The Nationwide Locator
PO Box 39903
San Antonio, Texas 78218
(210) 828-4667 Fax

Appendix C

Computer access programs

The Nationwide Locator also markets two computer access programs to locate missing people. These programs are for use by heir searchers, private investigators, collection agencies, attorneys, reunion planners, and others who are searching for a large number of people.

The Nationwide Locator Direct Access Package is a low-cost program that lets you enter the finest database in the country through which you can obtain addresses of people at the lowest possible price. There are no restrictions to who can use the Nationwide Locator Direct Access Package. The database does not provide any credit information or reports. None of the provided information is regulated by the Fair Credit Reporting Act. This access package includes six major categories of searches:

Social Security trace

Social Security number retrace (criss-cross)

Subject verification
Address verification
Telephone number ownership

All your searches are on-line and you receive instant responses. Most searches are $6 each. Social Security traces are less with volume usage.

No minimum usage requirements
No monthly user fee
No large up-front fee
No line charge
No sales tax
Instant reports
24-hour-a-day access
User-friendly access program

An IBM compatible computer, a modem, a telephone and a major credit card (VISA, MasterCard or American Express) are the only requirements. The cost of this package is $290.

The **NIS On-Line Information Services** is the nation's most versatile computer access package, and provides access to the files of all major information databases. This package is used by hundreds of private investigators, researchers and other professionals. Some of the available searches are:

Social Security searches
National criss-cross
Surname search
Surname searches
Address updates

Name and date-of-birth search
Postal forwarding
Commercial credit
Asset searches
Motor vehicle registration traces
Driver license traces
Criminal history
Worker's compensation
Numerous other on-line searches

The cost of each search varies. Most searches give you instant on-line results, while some searches will be returned within 3–5 days. You do not need a computer to use this program. It can be accessed by phone, fax or mail.

The NIS On-Line Information Services is user-friendly, menu driven, available 24 hours a day and accessible by phone, mail, fax and e-mail.

The cost of the Nationwide Locator Direct Access Package is $290. The cost of the NIS On-line Information Services is $395. You can be on-line within 3–5 days. For a brochure of either of these access programs, write or fax:

The Nationwide Locator
PO Box 39903
San Antonio, Texas 78218
(210) 828-4667 Fax

About the Author

Richard (Dick) S. Johnson served 28 years in the military and for the last 15 of those years was responsible for the locator service of two large Army commands. Dick retired from the Army in 1979 as a Lieutenant Colonel but his interest in locating people continued. For several years, he did extensive research on this subject. His expertise includes knowledge of records, manual search techniques as well as computer search techniques and databases.

In 1988, Dick authored the book *How to Locate Anyone Who Is or Has Been in the Military.* This unique book is now in its seventh edition. In 1994, he wrote *Find Anyone Fast by Phone, Fax, Mail and Computer.* Dick has operated the Nationwide Locator, a computerized locator service, since 1988.

He has personally solved thousands of difficult missing person cases involving relatives, birth parents, witnesses and heirs. He has made many family and military reunions possible, and has solved many difficult cases for the national and foreign media.

Today, Dick Johnson is a professional heir searcher and researcher. He has been responsible for locating hundreds of missing heirs who have received several million dollars in inheritances. He has solved cases that range in value from a few thousand dollars to millions of dollars.

He has appeared on hundreds of radio talk shows and numerous television programs including "The Ricki Lake Show," "Company" and "Case Closed."

Dick is the author of "Searching," a column that appears in *The Stars and Stripes, The National Tribune* newspaper and *Reunions* magazine. This column focuses on unique searches he has solved which have a great deal of human interest.

He currently lives in San Antonio, Texas with his wife, Mickey, and their dog, Ashley.

Bibliography

Barnhart, Clarence and Thorndike, E.L. *Thorndike Barnhart Intermediate Dictionary.* Scott, Foresman and Company, 1971.

Ferris, Charles J. "Billions in Unclaimed Funds Sit in State Treasuries—This is how to retrieve what's there for you." *Money,* February, 1989: 133

Fletcher, Marla. "Lost Money." *Canadian Consumer,* November, 1987: 34-36

Fritz, Michael. "Is Money Trying to Find You?" *Forbes,* April, 1988: 99

Fritz, Michael. "Loose Change." *Forbes,* April, 1988: 102

Lalli, Frank. "Playing Lost and Found with Your Money." *Money,* January, 1994: 7

Nelson, Phil. "Money for the Asking." *The American Legion Magazine,* March, 1985: 16

Paulson, Morton C. "Unclaimed Cash: Could Some Be Yours?" *Changing Times,* November 1988: 41-45.

Ross, Alice. "Buried Treasure." *Off Duty,* July/August, 1988: 14-15

Sawaya, Zina. "Losers, Weepers." *Forbes,* August, 1992: 131

Sims, John. "$8 Billion Pie." *Money,* November, 1992: 87-88

Unknown. "FHA Mortgages—$58 Million in Unclaimed Refunds." *Consumer Reports,* October, 1990: 669

Unknown. "IRS Has Unclaimed Tax Refund Money." *Army Families,* Winter, 1993: 6

Weberman, Ben. "Finders Keepers." *Forbes,* March 1987: 90

Winter, Annette. "Forgotten Funds Pile Up in State Coffers." *Modern Maturity,* June/July, 1993

Winter, Annette. "Hidden Insurance Benefits." *Modern Maturity,* August/September, 1992: 77

Other Publications Available:

HOW TO LOCATE ANYONE WHO IS OR HAS BEEN IN THE MILITARY: ARMED FORCES LOCATOR GUIDE

1996—7TH EDITION

The author, Lt. Col. Richard S. Johnson is the foremost expert in the nation on locating people with a military connection. Over 75,000 copies of this book have been sold and readers have located thousands of people. The 7th edition is completely revised, updated and expanded. The foreword is provided by General William Westmoreland.

This book contains directories of:

U.S. Military Installations

U.S. Base/Post Locators

Army, Air Force, and Fleet Post Offices

U.S. Navy and Coast Guard Ships

Military and Veterans Organizations

Military Unit Reunion Associations

Here is some of the valuable information included:

How to obtain unit of assignment, home address and telephone number of any member of the Army, Navy, Air Force, Marine Corps, Coast Guard, the Reserve Components, and National Guard.

How to locate a current, former or retired member of the armed forces or reserve component.

How to locate any of 27 million living veterans.

How to obtain ship or unit histories.

How anyone can obtain copies of official military personnel records of current, former or deceased military members.

New chapters include: How to Locate Women Veterans and How to Verify a Person's Military Service.

Find Anyone Fast by Phone, Fax, Mail And Computer

The author, Richard S. Johnson, a nationally renowned expert on locating missing people, has brought together state-of-the-art methods necessary to find anyone quickly. This informative book describes hundreds of proven search techniques. It lists resources and assistance available from federal, state and local government agencies as well as business and private sources. Computer searches available to the public are described in detail.

The valuable information contained in this book includes:

- How to organize your search.
- How to gather information to begin your search.
- How to find important identifying information.
- How to use the information you obtain.
- How to obtain assistance from federal, state and local government agencies.
- How to determine if the person is deceased.
- Important laws that may affect your search.
- Computer searches available to you.
- Actual case studies, so you can see how other searches have been successful.

"The best and most organized book I have ever owned on locating missing people."
—Jim Kroes, Private Investigator & Former Federal Investigator

"...useful and insightful..."— *PI Magazine*

Bookstore

How to Investigate by Computer Book II by Ralph D. Thomas. A manual of the new investigative technology that gives sources and teaches to investigate by computer. Learn about hard-to-find sources of information and how to access them. 130 pages, $34.95.

The Sourcebook of Federal Courts, US District and Bankruptcy. The definitive guide to searching for case information at the local level within the federal court system. Provides complete information on how to obtain criminal and civil court records and bankruptcy files from federal courts. 420 pages, $36.00.

The Sourcebook of County Court Records. A national guide of over 5,600 repositories of courthouse records. Provides information to obtain copies of criminal, civil and probate court records. 1996 edition, 556 pages, $33.00.

The Sourcebook of County/Asset/Lien Records. A national guide to all county/city government agencies where real estate transactions, USS financing statements, and federal/state tax liens are recorded. 464 pages, $29.00.

The MVR Book Motor Service Guide. A national reference detailing and summarizing, in practical terms, the description, access procedures, regulations and privacy restrictions of driver and vehicle records in all states. Check this book before attempting to locate people through state driver license and MVR offices. 272 pages, $18.00.

The Sourcebook of State Public Records. This book explains how to obtain information at the state level for business records, liens and security interest records (UCC), criminal records, worker" compensation, vital records, MVR, occupational licensing, business names, and permits. 360 pages, $33.00.

Order Form

MIE PUBLISHING
PO Box 17118
Spartanburg, SC 29301
(800) 937-2133

Publication	Price	Qty	Amount
Find Anyone Fast	$14.95		
How To Locate...Military	19.95		
Other books:			

Total: $_____

South Carolina orders please add 5% sales tax. _____
Postage and handling   4.05
Please add $1.00 for each additional book. _____
(Please consult publisher for Int'l mail prices)
Total amount enclosed: $_____

_____ / ___ / _____
Visa, MasterCard, American Express Card   Expiration Date

_____
Name and Signature

_____
Address (Apartment Number)

_____
City, State, Zip Code

(___) _____
Telephone Number

We accept government purchase orders!
All books are mailed Priority Mail by the U.S. Post Office.
Please remit entire order form.

Glossary

Definitions are to words as used in this book.

Abandoned. Forsaken; deserted.

Abandonment period. Time that funds or property is held by an organization or institution before being turned over to the state.

Agent. A person, firm, etc., empowered to act for another; a representative of a government agency.

Agreement. A document between the potential rightful owner or heir and the heir searcher.

Attorney. Any person having the legal power to act for another; a lawyer.

Bank. An establishment for receiving or lending money.

Beneficiary. Anyone receiving benefits; a person named to receive an inheritance or income from an insurance policy.

Benefit. Payment made by an insurance company,

public agency, etc., usually during sickness or retirement.

Claim. To demand as rightfully belonging to one.

Claimant. One who claims a right to something—such as land, property, etc.

Contract. A document between the potential rightful owner or heir and the heir searcher.

Creditor. A person or entity to whom money is owed.

Credit union. A cooperative association for pooling savings of members and for making low interest loans to them.

Decedent. A person who has died.

Disbursement. Payment.

Dormant. Not active; inoperative.

Escheat. A) Reversion of property to the state in absence of legal heirs or other qualified claimants or B) property entering possession of the state by this process (revert or cause to revert to the state by escheat).

Estate. All the property, real or personal, owned by an individual.

Fiduciary. Holding or held in trust/ a trustee.

Financial organization. Any bank, trust company, savings and loan association, credit union, building and loan association or investment company.

Finder's fee. Legal compensation for professional services paid to an individual or organization to locate an asset that is unknown to the rightful owner or heir.

Genealogist. A person who studies the ancestry and lineage of families.

Heir. A person who receives or has the right to receive someone's estate after that person dies.

Heir searcher. An individual or a company who finds unclaimed money, then locates and notifies the rightful owner or legal heir.

Inherit. To receive property as an heir.

Inheritance. The estate transferred to an heir.

Inheritance tax. A tax levied by the state upon the beneficiaries that receive property of a deceased person.

Intangible assets. Assets that don't materially exist such as bank accounts, insurance, dividends, interest payments, etc.

Intestate. The condition of having made no will; it is said that someone with no will dies intestate.

Life insurance. Insurance in which a stipulated (contracted) amount is paid at the death of the insured.

List of accounts. The names of individuals who own assets that are currently held by a state Unclaimed Property Office. This list sometimes includes addresses and dollar amounts.

Next of kin. Closest living relative.

Notary public. An official authorized to certify or attest documents or take affidavits. Same as a Notary.

Power of Attorney. A written statement legally authorizing one person to act for another.

Probate. To establish officially the validity of a will. When it is proved to the satisfaction of the judge, it is received, filed, and recorded. It is then said to be admitted to probate or probated.

Probate court. Various state courts which have jurisdiction in the matter of proving wills, appointing executors and administrators, and supervising the administration of estates.

Property. Also referred to as a real or tangible property ownership; something owned, especially real estate, holdings.

Real estate. Land, including the buildings or improvements on it and its natural assets.

Reporter. A person who locates cases in probate courts.

Security deposit. Something given as a pledge of repayment.

Tangible assets. Material assets you can touch, such as land, buildings, etc.

Testate. Having a will. It is said someone who dies with a will is testate.

Will. The legal statement of a person's wishes about what shall be done with his property after death. It usually must be in writing.

Index

NOTES

<u>NOTES</u>